The Emotional Intelligence Activity Book

The Emotional Intelligence Activity Book

50 Activities for Developing EQ at Work

Adele B. Lynn

AMACOM

American Management Association

New York • Atlanta • Brussels • Buenos Aires • Chicago • London • Mexico City
San Francisco • Shanghai • Tokyo • Toronto • Washington, D.C.

Special discounts on bulk quantities of AMACOM books are
available to corporations, professional associations, and other
organizations. For details, contact Special Sales Department,
AMACOM, a division of American Management Association,
1601 Broadway, New York, NY 10019.
Tel.: 212-903-8316   Fax: 212-903-8083
Web site: www.amacombooks.org

This publication is designed to provide accurate and authoritative
information in regard to the subject matter covered. It is sold with the
understanding that the publisher is not engaged in rendering legal,
accounting, or other professional service. If legal advice or other
expert assistance is required, the services of a competent professional
person should be sought.

Library of Congress Cataloging-in-Publication Data

Lynn, Adele B.
    The emotional intelligence activity book : 50 activities for developing EQ at work /
Adele B. Lynn.
        p.   cm.
    Rev. ed. of: 50 activities for developing emotional intelligence.
    Includes index.
    ISBN 0-8144-7123-4 (pbk.)
    1. Emotional intelligence—Problems, exercises, etc.   2. Success in business—Problems,
exercises, etc.   I. Lynn, Adele B. 50 activities for developing emotional intelligence.   II.
Title.

    BF576.3 .L96   2002
    152.4'076—dc21
                                                                                2001041233

Printing number

    10 9 8 7 6 5 4 3 2 1

Contents

What Is Emotional Intelligence?   1

A Coach's/Trainer's Guide to Helping Leaders Improve Emotional Intelligence   5

How to Use This Guide and How Not to Use It   7

A Guide to the 50 Emotional Intelligence Activities   9

Suggested Training Formats   11

EQ #1   Champion or Chump   15

EQ #2   Importance Meter   19

EQ #3   Adding Fuel to the Importance Meter   25

EQ #4   Rank Order Your Employees   31

EQ #5   Ask for Feedback   37

EQ #6   Picture Yourself   41

EQ #7   Personality Contest   45

EQ #8   Music of Our Workplace   49

EQ #9   Coming Through   55

EQ #10   Open and Friendly Versus Friendship   61

EQ #11   Listening Habits   65

EQ #12   Genuine Listening   71

EQ #13   Tuning In to Our Employees   75

EQ #14   I Was Appreciated   79

EQ #15   A Grateful Heart   85

EQ #16   Gifts   91

EQ #17   Yes, But . . .   97

EQ #18   Common Mistakes With Gratitude   101

EQ #19   A Note of Thanks   107

EQ #20   Dumped On   113

EQ #21   Doing a Fair Share   119

EQ #22   The Boss's Fair Share   125

EQ #23   Action/Reaction   131

EQ #24   Take a Stand   135

EQ #25   I Value, We Value   141

EQ #26   Contribution Spirit Killers   147

EQ #27   You Expect Me to What?   151

EQ #28   Great Vision   155

EQ #29   My Vision   161

EQ #30   Inspiring Words   165

EQ #31   Sharing Your Vision   169

EQ #32   Who Invents?   173

EQ #33   Visions Apply to People Too   179

EQ #34   Vision Spirit Killers   185

EQ #35   Advice From the Pros   189

EQ #36   Working Toward the Vision   193

EQ #37   Advice From Employees   197

EQ #38   Today's Actions Toward the Vision   203

EQ #39   Fuel the Vision   207

EQ #40   Picture Yourself   211

EQ #41   Lessons From Low Points/High Points   215

EQ #42   It's My Show   221

EQ #43   Interior Power   227

EQ #44   Control and Empowerment   231

EQ #45   Steps for Growth   237

EQ #46   Spirit Killers That Stunt Your Growth   243

EQ #47   Your Most Inspired Self   247

EQ #48   Your Leadership Coat of Arms   253

EQ #49   More Reflections   257

EQ #50   The Power of Pictures   261

Additional Ideas   265

EQ Activities for Developing Communication Skills   266

EQ Activities for Developing Team Building   267

EQ Activities for Developing Interpersonal Skills   268

EQ Activities for Developing Leaders/Managers/Supervisors   269

Recommended Resources   271

Index   273

The Emotional Intelligence Activity Book

What Is Emotional Intelligence?

The workplace need no longer linger in darkness regarding the factors leading to great performance. More than 25 years of research in the neurological field and specific study about the factors that contribute to success in the workplace have resulted in breaking through perceptions about intelligence. Quantifiable data on performance in a myriad of industries and organizations has resulted in a body of study called emotional intelligence (EQ). These years of study have named and identified the "intangibles" that predict success in the workplace. Emotional intelligence explains why, despite equal intellectual capacity, training, or experience, some people excel while others of the same caliber lag behind.

Repeatedly, we heard and told stories of people with intellectual brilliance often coupled with great experience and education who did not always produce the most capable leaders. Sometimes, even worse, these purveyors of knowledge and intellect created emotional disasters among their followers and plagued the halls of corporate America, dooming their followers to a work life of low creativity, minimal enthusiasm, low productivity, and even fear. And, of course, the corporate answer was "send them to a training class." Training classes almost always fell short because the training was not designed to get to the root of the matter and develop the core issue. Also, training was generically designed and was not targeted to the individual's own failure prescription.

Brilliant research by Daniel Goleman, Robert K. Cooper, Ayman Sawaf, and Robert E. Kelley have quantified the characteristics of emotional intelligence and allowed for measurement in a field that was before void of such measurement and definition. It is no longer an "accident" that certain competencies are found repeatedly in high performers. Many of these competencies are found in high performers at all levels, from customer service representatives to CEOs. No longer is the discussion about nonquantifiable "soft skills." Instead, we as trainers and coaches must find ways to build these talents that have been identified by these experts and labeled as emotional intelligence.

So, what exactly do the gifts of emotional intelligence comprise? For the answer to that question, I guide you back to the experts. Anyone who will be using this guide for coaching or training in the area of emotional intelligence must be completely familiar with the following works:

- *Working with Emotional Intelligence,* by Daniel Goleman
- *Executive EQ, Emotional Intelligence in Leadership and Organizations,* by Robert K. Cooper and Ayman Sawaf
- *How to Be a Star at Work,* by Robert E. Kelley

And for understanding the impact of emotional intelligence on workers and consistent language in this guide, I also refer you to my own work:

■ *In Search of Honor—Lessons from Workers on How to Build Trust,* by Adele B. Lynn

Although the language, models, and depth of this subject differ among the experts, the general thesis supported in these works is consistent. So, first and foremost, read the experts.

EMOTIONAL INTELLIGENCE—A WORKING DEFINITION

At the risk of oversimplifying, emotional intelligence is the dimension of intelligence responsible for our ability to manage ourselves and our relationships with others. Each day, both in our personal and business lives, opportunities and challenges present themselves. It is EQ that enables us to recognize and move toward the opportunity. And it is EQ that enables us to meet even the toughest of life's challenges.

EQ is the distinguishing factor that determines if we make lemonade when life hands us lemons or spend our life stuck in bitterness. EQ is the distinguishing factor that enables us to have wholesome, warm relationships, or cold, distant contacts. EQ is the distinguishing factor between finding and living our life's passions or just putting in time. EQ is the distinguishing factor that draws others to us or repels them. EQ is the distinguishing factor that enables us to work in concert and collaboration with others or to withdraw in dispute.

The competencies and gifts that EQ encompasses are many. Included are skills that drive our internal world as well as our response to the external one. Some examples include personal motivation; personal mastery over our life's purpose and intention; a well-honed timing for emotional expression and emotional control; empathy for others; social expertise that allows us to network and develop relationships that enhance our purpose; character and integrity that enable us to appear genuine and aligned; a tenacity to face and resolve both internal and external conflict; and personal influence that enables us to advance our purpose. EQ is a very valuable component of our functioning.

In the business world, however, so much of our emphasis has been placed on intellect. It has been on IQ and all of the analytical, factual, and measured reasoning power that IQ represents. Make no mistake, however; intellect has proven invaluable to drive our success in business. Financial decisions based on analytical details, sound strategies based on facts and data, and processes and procedures based on review and analysis are all critically important. However, to get to the next and higher level of competence in business, we must blend the progress that we've made in using intellect and IQ with the invaluable competencies of EQ. It is EQ that will solve our retention and morale problems, improve our creativity, create synergy from teamwork, speed our information by way of sophisticated people networks, drive our purpose, and ignite the best and most inspired performance from our followers.

The business case for EQ has already been made. In study after study, from many different industries and professions, those who had high EQ competencies outperformed their colleagues. Examples include the Air Force, which used emotional intelligence to select recruiters, resulting in a three-fold increase in their success and an immediate saving of $3 million annually; partners in a multinational consulting firm who were assessed on the

EQ competencies plus three others delivered $1.2 million more profit from their accounts than did other partners—a 139 percent incremental gain (Boyatzis, 1999); L'Oreal, whose sales agents selected on the basis of certain emotional competencies outsold their counterparts not selected on EQ competencies by $91,370, for a net increase of $2,558,360, and those selected on the basis of emotional competencies also had 63 percent less turnover during the first year than those selected in the typical way (Spencer & Spencer, 1993; Spencer, McClelland & Kelner, 1997). For a more comprehensive business case, refer to the experts at the Consortium for Research on Emotional Intelligence in Organizations, Cary Cherniss, Ph.D., Rutgers University.

Emotion is present in the workplace. Everyday. Everywhere. Emotion is energy. Learning to harness this energy and use it to impact the reasoning side of the business in a positive way is one of the great untapped resources yet to be conquered. Some leaders have done this successfully and have served as models to study. However, more leaders throughout the organization must learn to excel in this area in order to achieve the maximum benefit. Therefore, teaching EQ competencies throughout the organization is essential. This activity book is intended to help you get started on this essential path.

THE EQ FRAMEWORK

The information contained within these pages concentrates on developing some, but not all, aspects of emotional intelligence. (It is impossible for any 50 activities to ever effectively address the whole of this subject.) The exercises contained within these pages are aimed mostly at developing the following set of talents:

1. **Self-Awareness and Control**—This talent comprises two separate skills. The self-awareness component demands intimate and accurate knowledge of one's self and one's emotions. It also demands understanding and predicting one's emotional reactions to situations. One who is emotionally competent at self-awareness is also fully aware of one's values and core beliefs and knows the impact and effect of compromising these core components. The self-control component requires full mastery of being in control of one's emotions. Both positive and negative emotions are channeled in the most productive manner when one controls the emotion versus having the emotion control the person. The person with mastery and control of emotions can both anticipate and plan emotional reactions to maximize effectiveness.

2. **Empathy**—Empathy requires the ability to understand how others perceive situations. This perception includes knowing how others feel about a particular set of events or circumstances. Empathy requires knowing the perspective of others and being very able to see things from the value and belief system of the other person. It is the ability to fully immerse oneself in another's viewpoint, yet be able to remain wholly apart. The understanding associated with empathy is both cognitive and emotional. It takes into consideration the reasons and logic behind another's feelings or point of view, while also allowing the empathic party to feel the spirit of a person or thing.

3. **Social Expertness**—Social expertness is the ability to build genuine relationships and bonds with others that are based on an assumption of human equality. It allows people to genuinely express feelings, even conflict, in a way that builds rather than destroys relationships. Social expertness also enables a person to choose appropriate actions based on his or her feelings of empathy. The talent of social expertness allows caring, support, and concern to show for fellow humans in all of life's situations. Social expertness also demands that one read social situations for readiness, appropriateness, and spoken and unspoken norms. Resolving conflict without compromising core beliefs or values is an important component of social expertness. High social expertness also allows for strong networks on both a professional and personal level that can be enlisted readily when needed for aid.

4. **Personal Influence**—Personal influence is the ability to inspire others through example, words, and deeds. It is the ability to lead others by way of social expertness. Personal influence is the ability to read situations and exert influence and leadership in the desired direction. It is also the ability to confront issues that are important or debilitating to relationships, goals, missions, or visions. Personal influence is, in addition, exhibiting motivation for one's visions, missions, core values, and beliefs.

5. **Mastery of Vision**—Mastery of vision requires that the individual has the ability to set direction and vision guided by a strong personal philosophy. The ability to communicate and articulate with passion regarding direction and vision are also essential to mastery of vision. This talent serves as the inner compass that guides and influences one's actions. This inner compass also provides resilience and strength to overcome obstacles. It is the inner motivator and the guardian angel of our purpose. Mastery of vision allows us to know who we are and what we are compelled to do with our lives. When our actions and words are consistent with this personal philosophy, it is our sense of authenticity. When inconsistent, it is our sense of stress and discomfort.

A Coach's/Trainer's Guide to Helping Leaders Improve Emotional Intelligence

The coach/trainer's role is critical in helping employees develop emotional intelligence. Emotional intelligence is truly a lifetime journey. However, with the help of a coach or trainer, a six-month to one-year time period will provide a good beginning for an individual. Therefore, any organization that commits to building emotional intelligence must also commit to a long-term effort. It is the coach or trainer who can provide the consistent effort over this initial six-month to one-year time period for such growth to begin to occur. A long-term coach or trainer will also get to know the strengths, weaknesses, and areas of emotional intelligence that need the most work. In addition, growth will be well seeded if the leader is given ample feedback, reinforcement, and reminders to practice new behaviors on the job. This is the coach's or trainer's most golden role.

Step 1 Model emotional intelligence in all of your interactions with your participants.

Step 2 Assist employees in honest assessment. Assessment sources and methods can vary greatly. The coach/trainer must be able to ferret out the wheat from the chaff. Also, the coach/trainer must be familiar with each individual's situation to provide truth and honesty. The coach/trainer must also realize when someone's self awareness skills are not high enough to provide reliable data.

Step 3 Help employees reflect on their current philosophies/belief systems, and behaviors. Help them identify which belief systems and behaviors are helping them and which may be interfering with their effectiveness.

Step 4 Help workers set realistic objectives about changing destructive belief systems and behaviors. Also, show them how to change.

Step 5 Expose people to other ways of thinking. This could be through peers, books, mentors, or other masters.

Step 6 Challenge employees to create new belief systems and philosophies that will serve them and their colleagues in a better way.

Step 7 Help employees convert their belief systems or philosophies to productive behaviors. Encourage repetitive use of these new behaviors on the job.

Step 8 Provide and find others to provide positive reinforcement for the employees who are attempting to improve.

Step 9 Measure the results through assessment or other methods. Be sure to share the results with the employees.

Step 10 Mirror the behavioral results of changed belief systems and behaviors that improve followers' reactions. Celebrate and applaud the employees' efforts.

How to Use This Guide and How Not to Use It

- Assessment is an important phase of development for leaders. However, not all forms of assessment are created equal. As a trainer or coach, you must determine accuracy of assessment information. In addition, these methods require continuous assessment and feedback between you and the participants.

- Handpick selected exercises in this guide depending on the person or group that you are working with. In other words, select the exercises based on fit and appropriateness.

- The exercises in this guide are designed to be used as coaching tools. The coaching tools can be used in the classroom or in private coaching sessions. The tools are designed to help managers reflect on their leadership methods, practices, and philosophies, and then to use these reflections to guide their leadership behaviors.

- As the trainer or coach, you should use this guide with care and judgment. Not all managers are at the same level in their readiness to reflect and develop themselves. Therefore, we've coded the exercises with a High, Medium, and Low risk/difficulty factor.

- Also, you'll need to use care and judgment when considering offering these exercises in group settings or in private. Some organizational cultures do not promote an open atmosphere, and, therefore, the exercises may be more beneficial if used privately with the learner.

- We have, for your convenience, grouped some exercises or activities that work well together and suggest some sample training and modules for you to consider. Remember, however, that in group settings, not all participants will be at the same level. Therefore, it will be important for you to take this into consideration when planning the session.

- Do not use this guide as a substitute for all leadership development. Managers still will need basic skills in decision making, problem solving techniques, and methods related to strategic thinking, etc. However, the activities contained within these pages are essential for managers to flourish beyond these basic skills.

- Do supplement these activities with other training activities that will contribute to the learning. This is not, nor can it be, the only avenue to developing emotional intelligence.

- Recognize that your role as the coach or trainer in emotional intelligence is to act as a mirror for the learner. Sometimes, self-assessment in a leader with low self-awareness can be flawed, therefore, your role is expanded. You must hand to your learner the observations and insights from within and outside the classroom that facilitate his or her learning. Comments from employees, peers, and others must be part of the feedback that you give to assist the learner.

- As a coach or trainer in emotional intelligence, take care not to force people to participate if they aren't ready.

- Debriefing exercises are instrumental if progress it to be made in emotional intelligence. The questions at the end of each activity are designed to get participants to reflect on the learning. Please add questions that you believe will enhance the learning. Always ask the participant how the learning will result in changing his or her approach on the job.

- Remember basic information such as Myers-Briggs type and learning style information. Some people are introverted and will find reflection easy. Others are extroverted and will prefer to process the information by talking it through. As the coach or trainer, adjust your methods accordingly. Any exercise designed for private reflection on the following pages can easily be adapted.

- Exercises and activities aimed at increasing emotional intelligence demand that the learner internalize the information and then broaden or change his or her leadership philosophies. (Philosophies will result in changed behavior.) This cannot occur overnight. It is the trainer or coach's job to continuously keep this type of learning in front of the manager, to continuously challenge or affirm his or her philosophies that drive the leadership behavior.

- Don't expect Attila the Hun to be transformed into Gandhi. However, do expect progress. The key to progress in emotional intelligence is to continuously challenge the manager to rethink his or her philosophies that drive his or her management and then to support new behaviors related to this new thinking.

- Reinforcement of the new emotionally intelligent behavior is critical to acquiring the skill. The coach/trainer should reinforce these skills as often as possible. Ideally, the coach should also enlist the help of others within the organization, especially in a superior of the participant to also reinforce the behavior.

A Guide to the 50 Emotional Intelligence Activities

Emotional Intelligence Activity	Page Number	Risk/Difficulty	Emotional Intelligence Competencies				
			Self-Awareness/Control	Empathy	Social Expertness	Personal Influence	Mastery of Vision
1. Champion or Chump	15	M	✓		✓		
2. Importance Meter	19	L	✓	✓	✓		
3. Adding Fuel to the Importance Meter	25	L		✓	✓	✓	
4. Rank Order Your Employees	31	H	✓	✓	✓		
5. Ask for Feedback	37	H	✓	✓	✓		
6. Picture Yourself	41	L			✓		✓
7. Personality Contest	45	L	✓	✓	✓	✓	
8. Music of Our Workplace	49	M		✓	✓	✓	✓
9. Coming Through	55	H	✓	✓			
10. Open and Friendly Versus Friendship	61	M		✓	✓		✓
11. Listening Habits	65	M	✓	✓	✓		
12. Genuine Listening	71	L	✓	✓	✓		
13. Tuning in to Our Employees	75	M	✓	✓	✓		
14. I Was Appreciated	79	L	✓		✓	✓	
15. A Grateful Heart	85	L	✓		✓		
16. Gifts	91	L			✓	✓	
17. Yes, But . . .	97	M					✓
18. Common Mistakes With Gratitude	101	H	✓	✓		✓	
19. A Note of Thanks	107	H	✓	✓	✓	✓	
20. Dumped On	113	M		✓			✓
21. Doing a Fair Share	119	H		✓		✓	✓
22. The Boss's Fair Share	125	H	✓	✓		✓	
23. Action/Reaction	131	M	✓	✓		✓	
24. Take a Stand	135	H				✓	✓

Emotional Intelligence Activity	Page Number	Risk/Difficulty	Emotional Intelligence Competencies				
			Self-Awareness/ Control	Empathy	Social Expertness	Personal Influence	Mastery of Vision
25. I Value, We Value	141	M	✓			✓	✓
26. Contribution Spirit Killers	147	H	✓	✓		✓	
27. You Expect Me to What?	151	H	✓	✓		✓	
28. Great Vision	155	L	✓			✓	✓
29. My Vision	161	M			✓	✓	✓
30. Inspiring Words	165	H				✓	✓
31. Sharing Your Vision	169	M				✓	✓
32. Who Invents?	173	H	✓			✓	
33. Visions Apply to People Too	179	H	✓		✓	✓	
34. Vision Spirit Killers	185	H	✓	✓		✓	
35. Advice From the Pros	189	L	✓				✓
36. Working Toward the Vision	193	M				✓	✓
37. Advice From Employees	197	H	✓			✓	✓
38. Today's Actions Toward the Vision	203	M				✓	✓
39. Fuel the Vision	207	M	✓			✓	
40. Picture Yourself	211	M				✓	✓
41. Lessons From Low Points/High Points	215	H	✓			✓	
42. It's My Show	221	H	✓				✓
43. Interior Power	227	H	✓			✓	✓
44. Control and Empowerment	231	H	✓	✓		✓	
45. Steps for Growth	237	H	✓				✓
46. Spirit Killers That Stunt Your Growth	246	H	✓				✓
47. Your Most Inspired Self	247	H	✓				✓
48. Your Leadership Coat of Arms	253	H	✓				✓
49. More Reflections	257	H	✓				✓
50. The Power of Pictures	261	L	✓				✓

Suggested Training Formats

Suggested formats are simply designed to give you some idea of how to use/combine the exercises depending on your learning objectives. I would strongly suggest that you vary the formats depending on the makeup of the group. Also, supplement the formats with videos and other learning aids that support your objectives.

FORMAT A—INTRODUCTION TO EQ—½ DAY

Objectives: This session is designed as a primer to introduce some basic concepts of emotional intelligence. It is designed for leaders at any level who would like to learn more about how emotions impact the workplace. The participant will:

1. Learn that emotions are an integral part of everyone's work experience and are impacted by the leader

2. Learn about the impact between emotions and productivity and quality

3. Explore how and why the leader should find reasons to express gratitude in the workplace

4. Learn how to create a positive team environment through visuals

Icebreaker Activity/Introductions		15 min.
EQ #1	Champion or Chump	40 min.
EQ #15	A Grateful Heart	40 min.
EQ #16	Gifts	40 min.
Break		15 min.
EQ #50	The Power of Pictures	50 + 10 min. per person
Wrap-Up Summary		*15 min.*

FORMAT B—EQ ESSENTIALS—1 DAY

Objectives: This one-day workshop gives leaders some basic information about how emotions impact the workplace. It also explores how the leader's emotions impact his or her work team and equips the leader with some guidelines for addressing his/her emotions in the workplace. The participant will:

1. Learn that emotions are an integral part of everyone's work experience and are impacted by the leader

2. Learn the connection between emotions and productivity and quality

3. Lean how and why the leader should find reasons to express gratitude in the workplace

4. Identify his or her emotions in the workplace and the impact the emotions have on his or her team

5. Develop guidelines for expressing emotions that contribute to the overall productivity and quality of the team

Icebreaker Activity/Introductions		15 min.
EQ #1	Champion or Chump	40 min.
EQ #4	Rank Order Your Employees	50 min.
Break		15 min.
EQ #3	Adding Fuel to the Importance Meter	55 min.
Lunch		
EQ #15	A Grateful Heart	40 min.
EQ #16	Gifts	40 min.
Break		15 min.
EQ #9	Coming Through	85 min.
Wrap-Up Summary		*15 min.*

FORMAT C—EQ STRATEGIES—2 DAYS

Objectives: This two-day workshop gives leaders the basic groundwork about how emotions impact the workplace. It also explores how the leader's emotions impact his or her work team and equips the leader with some guidelines for addressing his/her emotions in the workplace. In addition, this workshop helps leaders to discover their core purpose and vision as it relates to being a leader. The participant will:

1. Learn that emotions are an integral part of everyone's work experience and are impacted by the leader

2. Learn that emotions impact productivity and quality output

3. Discover how and why the leader should find reasons to express gratitude in the workplace

4. Learn how to identify his or her emotions in the workplace and the impact the emotions have on his or her team

5. Develop guildelines for expressing emotions that contribute to the overall productivity and quality of the team

6. Explore his or her fundamental beliefs and values about leadership that drive his/her workplace behavior

7. Evaluate which beliefs and values contribute positively and negatively to his or her leadership approach

Day 1

Icebreaker Activity/Introductions		20 min.
EQ #1	Champion or Chump	40 min.
EQ #2	Importance Meter	65 min.
EQ #3	Adding Fuel to the Importance Meter	55 min.
Lunch		
EQ #15	A Grateful Heart	40 min.
EQ #16	Gifts	40 min.
Break		15 min.
EQ #9	Coming Through	85 min.
Wrap-Up Summary		*15 min.*

Day 2

EQ #28	Great Vision	50 min.
EQ #8	Music of Our Workplace	140 min.
Break		15 min.
EQ #29	My Vision*	30 min.
EQ #30	Inspiring Words*	40 min.
Lunch		
EQ #24	Take a Stand	45 min.
Break		15 min.
EQ #48	Your Leadership Coat of Arms	40 min. +5 min. per person
Wrap-Up Summary		*15 min.*

*Focus participants on only one aspect of vision—their vision for the type of team and culture that they would like to create within their work units.

EQ #1

Champion or Chump

EQ TARGET

✓	**Self-Awareness and Control**
	Empathy
✓	**Social Expertness**
	Personal Influence
	Mastery of Vision

OBJECTIVES

- To help participants become familiar with the past feelings that certain leaders fostered

- To determine exactly what those leaders did to foster certain feelings.

ESTIMATED TIME

40 minutes

MATERIALS

Emotional Intelligence Exercise #1

RISK/DIFFICULTY

Medium

COACHING TIPS FOR COACH/TRAINER

This EQ activity is designed to help participants realize the impact that the leader has on the follower. By reaching back into our memories of both positive and negative examples in our own work life, leaders can become sensitive to the power they have to influence and foster work environments. This EQ activity will build self-awareness by examining the individual's emotional environment.

Use this activity to begin a discussion of how significant it is for leaders to give followers a sense of importance and significance.

TRAINER'S/COACH'S NOTES

	APPROXIMATE TIME

1. Overview

1 minute

A. Explain to the individual or group that in order to gain high productivity, high creativity, or high quality, workers must believe that what they do is important. For most people, if they believe the task they are doing is not important, it is difficult, if not impossible, to give their full degree of commitment to that task.

B. Also explain to the group that not only the task must feel valued and significant, but the person doing the task must also feel valued, in order to bring out the best performance. "In addition to the task being important, it is your job as leaders, to create the kind of environment that also helps foster a sense of importance in the people doing the job."

2. Objective

1 minute

"The purpose of this exercise is to help you remember from your own storehouse of information and knowledge, times when a leader helped create a sense of significance or importance in you. In addition, this exercise will also help you remember times when you did not feel significant or important, and the impact that had on your desire to work to your full potential."

3. Give Directions

3 minutes

A. Give participants Exercise #1

B. Ask the participants to complete the table on the page by filling in specific examples of when they felt like a champion or like a chump. Ask them to think about specific bosses they have had and what exactly those bosses did to foster feelings of being a champion or chump.

C. Tell the participants to focus on actions that the boss took related to making them and their work feel important and significant.

D. Give the group or the individual some examples:

Examples of champion actions:

- I was told about the increased workload before I heard it from the grapevine.

- She always makes eye contact with me at staff meetings.

- She told the GM about my work.

Examples of chump actions:

- He didn't tell me they were going to phase out my unit. I heard it from the janitor.

- She never asks about my projects or tasks unless there is some time at the end of the meeting.

■ When I suggested an improvement, he immediately responded, "No way, we have other priorities." He didn't even listen to my suggestion.

E. Encourage the participants to think about both verbal and nonverbal messages that they have received.

F. Ask participants to complete the worksheet. Stay available to answer questions. **12 minutes**

4. Debrief the exercise with the following questions: **20 minutes**

A. What feelings did you have when your boss practiced "champion" actions?

B. What feelings did you have when your boss practiced "chump" actions?

C. Do you think these activities had any impact on your productivity? What about your creativity?

Emotional Intelligence Exercise 1

As you think about your past work experiences, when did you feel like a champion and when did you feel like a chump? Think about specific actions your boss took that contributed to your sense of importance or your lack of it. Some "champion" examples might be: He invited me to the morning meeting; she told me about the increased load before I heard it from the grapevine; she always makes eye contact with me at a staff meeting; she told the GM about my work. Some "chump" examples might be: She never looks at me in a meeting, but she addresses everyone else with her eye contact; he didn't tell me there was a major layoff coming, I learned it from the janitor; she never asks about my projects or tasks until the end of the meeting; when I suggested an improvement, he quickly said "no way, we have other priorities."

Champion	Chump

EQ #2

Importance Meter

EQ TARGET

✓	Self-Awareness and Control
✓	Empathy
✓	Social Expertness
	Personal Influence
	Mastery of Vision

OBJECTIVES

- To help participants recognize that they may unintentionally give different messages to their people regarding the importance of their job or task

- To visually represent where to place efforts in order to improve the level of importance that people experience in the workplace.

ESTIMATED TIME

65 minutes

MATERIALS

Emotional Intelligence Exercise #2

RISK/DIFFICULTY

Low

COACHING TIPS FOR COACH/TRAINER

This EQ activity is designed to help leaders know exactly where they must place their efforts in order to heighten their staff's sense of importance. The visual representation is a strong way to recognize how different employees may feel in regard to their sense of importance and significance in the work unit.

This activity will encourage leaders to regard followers as individuals. Also, it will help leaders know what to give each follower so that they can do their best.

Leaders with high EQ have highly developed radar that helps them to sense the feelings and perspectives of others. This exercise helps develop that radar by asking the participant to imagine things from the employee's perspective.

It is common for participants to offer rationalizations as to why an employee's "Importance Meter" might be low. It is critically important for you to reinforce that this exercise is about empathy, to see it from the employee's perspective. Therefore, any rationalizations will interfere with the leader's ability to empathize.

TRAINER'S/COACH'S NOTES

	APPROXIMATE TIME
1. Overview	**2 minutes**

1. Overview

A. Explain to the individual or group that it is possible to give certain individuals or tasks higher priority and importance in the workplace. Without realizing this, leaders may unintentionally create negative caste feelings that divide the work group. "Each day, you are given multiple opportunities to either confirm or negate the importance of our employees' work. For example, if we pay close attention to one person and little to another, this could be interpreted as seeing the work of the second person as unimportant."

B. Also explain that as a leader, it is important to manage how much significance you place on the work of your people. It is also important to strive for a sense that all work is important. Whether the person is the janitor or the CEO, they should be made to believe that their work is significant.

2. Objective   **1 minute**

"The purpose of this exercise is to think about each person who works for you. Then, to demonstrate visually (1) how much importance you place on each person's task and (2) how much importance you place on each person doing the task."

3. Give Directions   **3 minutes**

A. Give the participants Exercise #2

B. Ask the participants to list each person on their staff and write their name on the line to the left of the importance meter.

C. Ask the participants to consider what they do each day to help that person realize that he/she and his/her task are of importance.

D. Instruct the participants to draw a line on the meter to the right that would indicate the level of importance they give each person in their group.

E. As an example, ask the group to consider things such as:

(1) How often do you ask about their work?

(2) Are their concerns about their job high on your priority list, or low?

(3) When was the last time you asked this person for an opinion about work?

(4) Is this person first or last to hear from you about important developments in the workplace?

F. Coach the participants to be careful of rationalization. Explain that rationalizations will get in the way of empathy. The trainer must model empathy during this discussion. For example, explain that you understand that the participants have many demands on and priorities for their time and that sometimes it is hard to give people the attention they would like to.

G. Ask the participants to complete the worksheet. Stay available to answer questions. **10–20 minutes**

4. **Debrief the exercise with the following questions:** **40 minutes**

    A. Are your employees filled up or running on empty?

    B. Why did you place some people's importance meter lower than others?

    C. What influence do you think you have on a person's importance scale?

    D. What actions do you think would increase a person's scale?

    E. What actions do you think would lower a person's scale?

    F. What do you think would happen if all employees were running on "Empty?"

    G. What do you think would happen if all employees were running on "Full?"

    H. Besides your activities as the leader, who else impacts a person's importance scale?

    I. Who else can you influence to help impact a person's importance scale positively?

NOTE: During the debriefing, be sure to encourage the leader to realize that certain people may feel insignificant despite the leader's efforts. Also encourage the leader to try to influence the employee's sense of importance and significance. It's the right thing to do, even if the results are not the same with everyone.

OPTIONS: If you are using this exercise with a group, break the participants in small groups of three or four. Then, on the flip chart, list three or four of the debriefing questions listed above. Ask each small group to discuss the questions.

Emotional Intelligence Exercise 2

If each of your employees had a gauge, or indicator, so that you could see the amount of importance you place on him or her in your workplace, what would their indicator read? Write each employee's name to the left, then draw a line marking the level of "importance" you give to each person on the gauge to the right. Are your employees filled up, or are they running on empty?

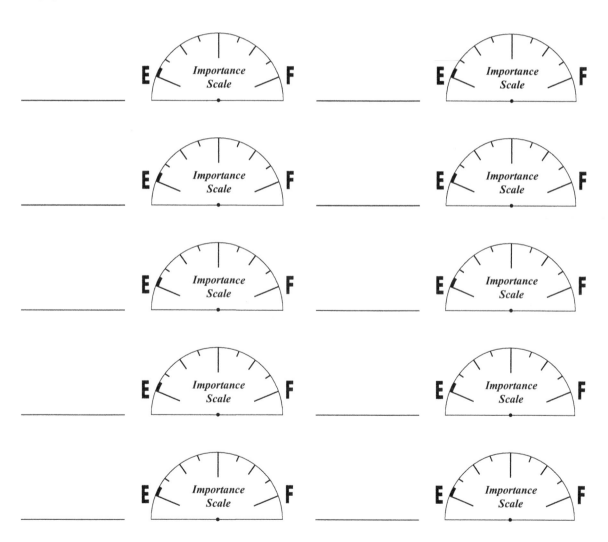

EQ #3

Adding Fuel to the Importance Meter

EQ TARGET

	Self-Awareness and Control
✓	**Empathy**
✓	**Social Expertness**
✓	**Personal Influence**
	Mastery of Vision

OBJECTIVES

■ To help participants recognize how each of their employees receive individual messages regarding the importance of their job or task

■ To help participants determine influence and leadership strategies that will increase people's sense of importance

■ To increase the sense of relationship/bonding that will occur between leader and follower.

ESTIMATED TIME

55 minutes

MATERIALS

Emotional Intelligence Exercise #3

RISK/DIFFICULTY

Low

COACHING TIPS

This EQ activity is designed to help leaders identify specific ways to influence and inspire followers. It is essential for each follower to feel valued. The social expertness of leaders determines how well they can build bonds and influence followers. Leaders who have this EQ skill also know that this is a continual part of their leadership role.

This exercise is aimed at generating concrete ideas to bolster people's sense of importance related to the work they do. It is important to coach the leaders to be as specific as possible. The result of this exercise should be specific actions, not vague expressions. For example, a good result would be "I will stop by Mary's desk and ask her about her ideas for the newsletter next week." A poor result would be, "I will help Mary feel important." The latter is too vague and has little chance of leading to any change on the part of the leader.

TRAINER'S/COACH'S NOTES

	APPROXIMATE TIME

1. Overview — 2 minutes

A. Explain to the individual or group that emotional intelligence can be translated to behaviors on the job. The leader with high emotional intelligence acts in ways that influence followers. Giving followers a strong sense of importance is essential to good leadership. Explain that there is no set pattern for the leader to do this, instead, the leader must hand craft actions that will fuel a sense of importance in his/her employees. Also explain that each employee is different and therefore will respond to different actions. "In order to get the fullest commitment possible from your employees, as leaders you must find ways that help each employee to feel significant. It is your role as the leader to add fuel to your employee's "Importance Meter.""

2. Objective — 1 minute

"The purpose of this exercise is to help you identify specific ways to influence and inspire your followers by bolstering their sense of importance. The goal of this exercise is for you to come up with very concrete actions that you think will help your employees feel important, because employees who feel important are more apt to be productive and creative. However, each employee is different, and, therefore, it will take different actions for each employee."

3. Give Directions

A. Give the participants Exercise #3

B. Ask the participants to list each employee's name on the worksheet.

C. After each employee's name, ask the participant to list a few specific actions that the participant could take to contribute to that person's sense of importance.

D. Instruct the participants to consider two types of actions:

(1) Actions aimed at making the person feel valued and

(2) Actions aimed at making the person's tasks have value. Especially, spend some time considering some of the mundane tasks that employees are asked to do. Participants should ask themselves how they could bolster the importance of these tasks.

E. Give participants some examples and instruct them to be very specific. Examples include:

(1) I will talk to Mary next week about ideas for the newsletter.

(2) I will ask Joe to report on the improvements he has made to the operating system at the next staff meeting.

(3) I will let Harriet know that a customer is coming in next week, and I

will ask her if she would be willing to give the customer an overview of the processing area.

(4) At the next staff meeting I will let the staff know the status of the XYZ project in an adjacent department.

F. Ask participants to complete the worksheet. Stay available to answer questions.   **15–20 minutes**

G. Ask participants to form a team of four and share some examples of the actions that were written in the exercise. Ask each group to share several actions that individuals wrote. Be sure to coach for specific examples. Also, encourage participants to listen for ideas that might benefit some of the employees on their list, and to add beneficial ones to their list.   **15 minutes**

4. **Debrief the exercise with the following questions:**   **20 minutes**

A. Give some examples of specific actions you wrote.

B. Why is it important to come up with specific actions for each of your employees?

C. What can you do to elevate mundane tasks?

D. What benefit do you derive from writing down specific actions you could take to bolster your employees' sense of importance?

E. What benefit will you receive if you implement these actions?

F. What benefit will your employees receive if you implement these actions?

G. When do you intend to implement these actions?

Emotional Intelligence Exercise 3

For each person on your staff, write specific ways in which you could add fuel to their sense of importance. What could you do that would contribute to people's sense of importance? What could you do to elevate even the most mundane tasks?

_____

_____

_____

_____

_____

_____

_____

_____

_____

_____

_____

_____

_____

_____

EQ #4

Rank Order Your Employees

EQ TARGET

✓	**Self-Awareness and Control**
✓	**Empathy**
✓	**Social Expertness**
	Personal Influence
	Mastery of Vision

OBJECTIVES

- To help participants recognize that they may hold certain positions/people in higher status than others within the work group

- To help participants determine if this status may indeed be visible on some level to employees

- To improve participants' awareness of the messages they may send to higher status and lower status employees

- Through awareness, this exercise will help lead participants to greater self control in their interactions with people and improve empathy.

ESTIMATED TIME

50 minutes

MATERIALS

Emotional Intelligence Exercise #4

RISK/DIFFICULTY

High

COACHING TIPS

Sometimes, intentionally or unintentionally, all leaders rank order employees. Some organizations even give salary increases based on some type of ranking system. Ranking may cause problems for the leader. For example, the leader may consciously or unconsciously send negative messages to the people on the bottom of the ranking. These messages may inadvertently cause people to believe they are not important or valued to the organization. This can spiral into additional performance problems.

The caution for the leader is to recognize that he values employees differently, but the leader must employ self-restraint to be sure that he is not giving messages that counter productivity.

For example, if a leader does not value a certain job function but instead views it as a necessary evil that he must contend with, that leader is apt to give the employee performing this function less time, less patience, less praise, fewer development opportunities, and even less pay even though the employee may be doing a fine job.

In another example, a leader may have a situation where two people are doing the same job but one employee is outperforming the other. In this case, the leader may inadvertently give the good performer more information, may stop for more informal conversations, or may otherwise send status messages that could cause further decline in the performance of the second employee.

The leader with high empathy knows that his actions can cause status issues within a group. This leader works hard to employ self-restraint and contain his enthusiasm for one employee at the expense of devaluing another's morale.

This exercise helps the leader recognize that he probably has a "mental" rank order that may affect his relationships with the employees. It also helps the leader to develop awareness and empathy skills, by examining his interactions with employees.

TRAINER'S/COACH'S NOTES

	APPROXIMATE TIME

1. Overview

Explain to the individual or group that building trust and strong bonds with employees requires leaders to be aware of the verbal and nonverbal messages they send to employees. In order for a leader to inspire followers, these messages must contain elements that give followers a sense of importance and value. Explain that sometimes leaders inadvertently give messages that signal counter emotions.

2 minutes

2. Objective

"The purpose of this exercise is to help you identify known and unknown factors that may cause you to send signals to employees suggesting you value one over another. The goal of this exercise will be for you to rank order your employees and then examine if you send different messages to the people on the top of the ranking versus the people on the bottom of the ranking. We will also explore the impact of this on employee morale."

1 minute

3. Give Directions

A. Give the participants Exercise #4.

B. Ask the participants to focus their attention to part 1 of the handout. Ask the participants to rank order each employee by name on the worksheet in sequential order of whose job they value most to least. Coach participants to think in terms of the job the employee performs, not the employee's performance or abilities. Ask how important the job duties are that this person performs.

C. Now, ask participants to focus their attention to part 2 of the handout. Ask the participants to rank order each employee by name on the worksheet ranking job performance. Ask whose job performance is the best and whose is the worst.

D. Instruct the participants to analyze their interactions with the people on the top of the list and those on the bottom. Consider the following:

    (1) Who is more likely to receive discretionary information (information not necessary to the person's job), but broader information about the department or organization?

    (2) Is there any difference in the amount of casual conversations you have with people on the top of the ranking versus those at the bottom of the ranking?

    (3) Whom do you think of first when you have an important assignment? Whom do you give the assignment to?

    (4) Have training opportunities or other "perks" been distributed fairly in the opinion of the employees?

(5) What other actions could you have taken, that may be perceived as devaluing, to the people on the lower end of the rankings?	**5 minutes**
NOTE: It is important to coach participants to realize that the purpose of this exercise is to sensitize the participants and develop empathy for the point of view of the people on the bottom of the scale. It is NOT appropriate for the trainer to make judgments about the participants' actions. The trainer/facilitator should only serve as a mirror to allow the participants to decide if their actions or decisions could cause unintentional status or division in the work group.	**15–20 minutes**
4. **Debrief this exercise by assigning participants to groups of four.** Within the groups, ask participants to share at least one insight that they learned from analyzing the data. If coaching an individual, ask the individual to share insights.	**20 minutes**

Emotional Intelligence Exercise 4

Quickly rank order your employees in terms of whose job you value most to least. Which job do you consider most important to you and the functioning of your department or area? What subtle messages might you send to the people near the bottom of the list?

_____

_____

_____

_____

_____

_____

_____

For each person on your staff, quickly rank order your employees in terms of whose job performance you consider to be the best to that person whose job performance you consider to be the worst. What subtle messages might you send to the people near the bottom of the list?

_____

_____

_____

_____

_____

_____

_____

_____

EQ #5

Ask for Feedback

EQ TARGET

✓	Self-Awareness and Control
✓	Empathy
✓	Social Expertness
	Personal Influence
	Mastery of Vision

OBJECTIVES

- To help participants develop a greater awareness of their employees' perceptions
- To help participants gain a greater awareness of their strengths and weaknesses
- To improve relationships and bonds with employees by genuinely listening to their perceptions.

ESTIMATED TIME

60 minutes

MATERIALS

Emotional Intelligence Exercise #5

RISK/DIFFICULTY

High

COACHING TIPS FOR COACH/TRAINER

Accurate feedback is essential for emotional intelligence. Feedback from a variety of sources is important to ensure balance and accuracy. Therefore, self assessment, 360-assessments, blind employee opinion surveys, and individual feedback sessions with employees are all important forms of assessment that improve the leader's self-awareness.

This exercise is aimed at gaining individual feedback from employees. The leader sits face to face with the employee and asks specific interview questions aimed at improving the leader's self-awareness while at the same time working to strengthen the bonds with the employee by practicing effective listening skills.

Readiness is always a factor to consider when implementing any type of learning activity. This activity has some great rewards and also some risks attached. Therefore, you must take extreme care in positioning this exercise.

First, you should only ask participants to perform this exercise if you believe they have a high level of reflective listening skills. Second, if you have any reason to believe that any participant may harbor resentment if presented with negative feedback by an employee, do not jeopardize the employee by asking the participant to perform this exercise. Third, you should assess the degree to which the participant is willing to act on the feedback. If you believe the participant is ready to make some behavior changes, then this exercise could be a very powerful catalyst for change. Be sure to make yourself available for individual coaching after this exercise.

TRAINER'S/COACH'S NOTES

	APPROXIMATE TIME

1. Overview

Explain to the individual or group that one of the most important tools for strengthening emotional intelligence is accurate self-assessment. Feedback from a variety of different sources is the best means of developing a well-balanced and accurate assessment. Also explain that when the conditions are right, face-to-face honest feedback is a very powerful tool to gain insight into how leaders come across. Sometimes, getting this feedback is as simple as asking the right questions.

1 minute

2. Objective

"The purpose of this exercise is to help you gain information from your employees that will help you to become a better leader. The information that you will gain is related to how well you are able to create an environment in which your employees feel significant and valued. When employees feel significant and valued, you can expect greater productivity, creativity, and quality. The method that you will use will be to simply sit down and ask your employees for their input."

1 minute

NOTE: It is wise to provide a refresher on reflective/active listening before presenting this exercise.

15 minutes

3. Give Directions

A. Give the participant(s) Exercise #5.

B. Ask each participant to ask her employees if they would be willing to meet to answer some questions. The leader should explain that she would like some feedback so that she can become a better leader.

C. Coach leaders to practice reflective and active listening during the interview process.

D. Allow leaders time to implement the interviews.

4. Debrief and discuss the interview results with each participant. Debrief using the following questions:

40 minutes

A. What did you learn that supported your own perceptions?

B. What did you learn that surprised you?

C. What would you like to change based on the information that you learned/relearned?

D. What was your greatest insight? Why?

Emotional Intelligence Exercise 5

In practice, actions speak louder than words. Therefore, as a leader, it's important to assess the messages you send to your employees. Sometimes the best way to know what your employees are thinking is to ask. If you feel comfortable, explain to your employees that you would like their help in becoming a better leader. Ask each employee the following questions:

1. What would you like to be included in that you currently feel excluded from?

_____

_____

_____

2. How do I view your tasks in relation to the other people in this department? Do you think I treat them as less important or more important?

_____

_____

_____

3. What have I done to elevate your sense of importance at work?

_____

_____

_____

4. How have I diminished your sense of importance at work?

_____

_____

_____

EQ #6

Picture Yourself

EQ TARGET

	Self-Awareness and Control
	Empathy
✓	Social Expertness
	Personal Influence
✓	Mastery of Vision

OBJECTIVES

- To help participants visualize themselves in successful situations
- To encourage participants to act on their thoughts
- To build successes with employees by visualizing actions that are consistent with the goal of building employees' sense of importance.

ESTIMATED TIME

90 minutes

MATERIALS

Emotional Intelligence Exercise #6

RISK/DIFFICULTY

Low

COACHING TIPS FOR COACH/TRAINER

The ultimate point of training or coaching is to get the participant to act in a way that will produce the desired result with the employee. One step that is often assumed, yet not always realized, is that the leaders can picture themselves successfully implementing the desired behavior. This visualization step precedes action. Therefore, it is very important to eventual behavior change on the part of the participant.

This exercise offers a mental rehearsal of the desired actions. It allows participants to prepare themselves so that when the situation and opportunity occur, the desired behaviors will follow.

Motivation for reaching goals is a critical part of emotional intelligence. Visualization is an important step in creating the motivation for successfully implementing a goal.

TRAINER'S/COACH'S NOTES

	APPROXIMATE TIME

1. Overview — *1 minute*

Explain to the individual or group that one of the most important components of emotional intelligence is motivation to act on one's goals. Emotional competence is characterized by the ability to initiate positive actions toward goals and maintain motivation and optimism despite roadblocks. Explain that rehearsal is a very important part of success. Just as people would prepare themselves for a job interview or a presentation to senior management, leaders should prepare themselves for positive interactions with their employees.

2. Objective — *1 minute*

"The purpose of this exercise is to help you visualize yourself in positive actions and words with your employees. These positive actions will be related to giving your employees a sense of importance aimed at both the tasks your employees perform and also building the sense of significance with the employees. It is important to develop this sense of significance with employees each and every day."

3. Give Directions — *60 minutes*

    A. Give the participants Exercise #6.

    B. Ask each participant to think about each of his employees. Visualize a typical workday and the interactions you have with your employees each day.

    C. Imagine yourself as an expert who knows exactly what to do and say to give people a sense of significance and to help employees see the value in the tasks they perform each day.

    D. What could you do or say to each employee that would add to his sense of significance?

    E. For each employee who reports to you, imagine having this conversation or taking some action to bolster his/her sense of importance. What exactly would you say or do? Where would you be when you are having this conversation or taking this action? Listen to your voice. How does it sound? What is your body language suggesting?

    F. Ask the participants to repeat this visualization for each employee.

    G. Participants should take notes for each visualization, and write down exactly what they would say or do, what they look like, sound like, etc.

    H. Ask participants to indicate a date on which they will talk to each of their employees.

4. Debrief — *30 minutes*

    A. Follow up with participants to determine if they acted on their visualizations. Ask them to report what went well and what did not produce the desired result. Discuss why.

Emotional Intelligence Exercise 6

Picture yourself. As you think about the idea of giving importance and significance to the people and the tasks they perform in the workplace, imagine yourself as a true expert in this area. As this great expert, what would you picture yourself doing every day with each of your employees? Get creative and imaginative. What do your pictures look like? Make a list below that describes how you will give your employees a sense of importance and how you will elevate the importance of their tasks. These should be specific things you can picture yourself doing in your workplace starting right now.

Name _____
I will bolster this employee's sense of significance in the following ways:

_____

_____

_____

Name _____
I will bolster this employee's sense of significance in the following ways:

_____

_____

_____

Name _____
I will bolster this employee's sense of significance in the following ways:

_____

_____

_____

EQ #7

Personality Contest

EQ TARGET

✓	**Self-Awareness and Control**
✓	**Empathy**
✓	**Social Expertness**
✓	**Personal Influence**
	Mastery of Vision

OBJECTIVES

- To improve relationships and bonds with employees by heightening awareness of how leaders' perceptions affect their relationships

- To help participants improve motivation and inspiration levels for all employees

- To help participants realize that they may indeed be sending visible messages to employees that tell them they are not equal.

ESTIMATED TIME

75 minutes

MATERIALS

Emotional Intelligence Exercise #7

RISK/DIFFICULTY

Low

COACHING TIPS FOR COACH/TRAINER

Leaders are people too. Therefore, they often like certain people more than others. However, when those certain people happen to work for them, others in the group may perceive this as unfair, practicing favoritism, or other undesirable leadership behaviors that are counter to productivity.

So, the most important first step is to recognize that leaders like certain employees more than others. This awareness is important and will be the first step in recognizing that the leader must be careful not to create an environment that creates negative perceptions.

For example, if a leader finds employee A to be exhaustive, boring, or just plain annoying, the leader probably avoids or otherwise spends less time and attention with this employee. Sometimes too, the leader may just find the person's values offensive or otherwise disagree with the person's lifestyle. These feelings on the part of the leader may be influencing the way the leader interacts with the person on work-related issues. On the other hand, if employee B has similar values, has an interesting personality, or otherwise has qualities that the leader just plain likes, the leader may very well be treating this person with some unspoken priority.

The purpose of this exercise is to recognize that our personal feelings toward employees may set up a ranking system that interferes with our ability to lead. In addition, the exercise is designed to improve self-awareness and empathy skills of the leader.

TRAINER'S/COACH'S NOTES

	APPROXIMATE TIME
1. Overview Explain to the individual or group that one of the most important tools for strengthening emotional intelligence is accurate self-awareness. Being aware of one's feelings as a leader will help the leader to be able to evaluate the fairness of her actions. This emotional honesty can lead to greater self-control when faced with situations that "press our hot button" or otherwise cause an emotional reaction. Stress that all leaders, first, are human, and, therefore, are subject to normal and natural emotions when working with people.	**2 minutes**
2. Give Directions A. Give the participants Exercise #7 B. Ask each participant to rank order her employees based solely on personality. Ask the participant, "Which employees do you like the most? Which employees do you like the least? Consider whom you enjoy just shooting the breeze with and whom you prefer to avoid. Rank order your employees from most likable to least likable." C. Coach leaders to be honest about this. Encourage leaders to recognize that it is natural for them to have preferences. D. Allow leaders time to rank order their employees. E. Now, instruct participants to answer the following questions on the worksheet: (1) Is there a difference in the amount of casual conversation time that you spend with the employees at the top of the list versus the bottom of the list? Explain. (2) Is there a difference in your body language when you interact with the employees at the top of the list versus the employees on the bottom? Explain. (3) Is there a difference in the mental thoughts that you have when people approach you who are at the top of the list versus people from the bottom? Explain.	**40 minutes**
3. Debrief and discuss the questions on the worksheet with the participants. You can also pair participants to discuss their insights with other participants in the class. In general discussion, ask the participants the following: (1) Do you think employees are sometimes attuned to these subtle differences? Explain. (2) Why, as leaders, should you be concerned about whether or not employees are aware of these subtle differences? **NOTE:** Statistically more than 70 percent of what we communicate is nonverbal according to a 1996 UCLA study.	**30 minutes**

Emotional Intelligence Exercise 7

Quickly rank order your employees in terms of whom you like the most. That's right. Be honest. Whom do you like the most as a person? Whom do you like the least? We aren't asking about performance or productivity, just plain personality. What subtle messages might you send to the people on the bottom of the list that may communicate that you don't like them as much as you like some of their coworkers?

_____

_____

_____

Reflect on the following:
Is there a difference in the amount of time you spend in casual conversation with the people on the top of the list versus the people on the bottom? Please explain.

_____

_____

_____

Is there a difference in your body language when relating to the people on the top of the list versus the people on the bottom? Please explain.

_____

_____

_____

Is there a difference in the "mental chatter" that you experience with the people on the top of the list versus the people on the bottom? Mental chatter is the conversation that goes on in your mind about a particular person or situation. An example of mental chatter: "Oh no, here comes Susie; what is she going to complain about now?" Please explain.

_____

_____

_____

EQ #8

Music of Our Workplace

EQ TARGET

	Self-Awareness and Control
	Self-Awareness and Control
✓	Empathy
✓	Social Expertness
✓	Personal Influence
✓	Mastery of Vision

OBJECTIVES

- To help participants verbalize the culture they perceive in their work units or departments by using music as a metaphor
- To encourage participants to try to shape their workplace culture by using music as a metaphor
- To encourage participants to verbalize to their employees their vision of a perfect workplace culture
- To open the lines of communication with employees and leaders regarding the underlying culture of their workplace.

ESTIMATED TIME

140 minutes

MATERIALS

Emotional Intelligence Exercise #8

RISK/DIFFICULTY

Medium

COACHING TIPS FOR COACH/TRAINER

Music can be a fun and safe way for people to talk about the workplace environment. Within different types of music, one can find just about every imaginable tempo and mood. Just as music is different, each workplace is different and has its own mood and tempo. Some workplace environments feel and sound like a John Phillips Sousa march, while others feel more like a funeral march. Still others resonate with the sound of the blues.

The first step is to use music as a metaphor for recognizing and discussing the different moods and tempos of the workplace. Next, it is helpful for leaders to recognize the power they have to influence the mood and tempo of the workplace.

The ultimate point of this exercise is to get leaders to visualize and communicate culture changes that would improve the workplace and create an environment most conducive to creativity, productivity, and quality.

When coaching, realize that some leaders will respond to the music and others will respond more to the lyrics. In either case, both are powerful symbols and can be fruitful when discussing workplace culture.

TRAINER'S/COACH'S NOTES

	APPROXIMATE TIME

1. Overview

Explain to the individual or group that the ability to "tune into" the workplace culture is an extremely important component of emotional intelligence. Being able to read a situation and determine the political inferences is important. This skill requires empathy and the ability to read the group's energy. Emotional competence is characterized by the ability to first distinguish the feelings of the individuals and the group and then to initiate positive actions toward influencing and leading the group toward desired goals.

1 minute

2. Objective

"The purpose of this exercise is to help you identify your workplace culture through the metaphor of music. In music, a variety of moods and tempos abound. That's also true in your workplaces. I'm sure you've walked into some meetings where it feels like *The Flight of the Bumble Bee* and others where it feels like *Take This Job and Shove It.* Through music, you can assess your workplace and provide some insights into the culture that drives your department. Also through music, you can begin to visualize or 'hear' a more perfect workplace culture."

2 minutes

3. Give Directions

A. Give the participants Exercise #8.

B. Tell the participants that you are about to play several clips of music. When they hear the clip, they are to think about and describe the kind of work atmosphere that the clip most likely signifies to them and write a description on their worksheet.

C. Play several clips of music. Some suggestions would be:

  (1) A fast intense piece of music such as *The Flight of the Bumble Bee*

  (2) A funeral march or other somber and slow music selection

  (3) A joyful, fun-filled piece of music that conveys upbeat, positive moods and fast yet controlled tempos

  (4) A chaotic, mixed-up, unharmonious selection that implies chaos and frantic unplanned actions

D. After you have played each selection, allow the participants a few moments to write down their description.

E. Replay the first selection and ask the participants to describe the kind of work situation that they associated with the clip. Allow for discussion. Ask, "How would it feel to work in a constant state of this melody?"

F. Repeat for all the other selections.

50 minutes

10 minutes

20 minutes

G. Now ask participants to "compose" in their heads the perfect music for a workplace. What does it sound like? Ask them to team up with a partner and describe the sound of their perfect workplace.   **10 minutes**

H. Now ask each participant to tune into his or her actual department music and try to describe the music that is heard.   **5 minutes**

I. Ask partners to share the difference between the actual and the ideal workplace music.

4. Debrief the full group with the following questions: **40 minutes**

A. If your workplace were music, what kind of music would it be and why?

B. What music is your corporate band playing?

C. What instrument do you play?

D. Are you in tune? In rhythm? Please elaborate.

E. How much influence does the leader have over the workplace music?

F. What can you do to influence the "music" in your workplace?

Variation: **Name That Tune**

1. If the participants would like some feedback from their employees, they can ask employees to name a song that best describes and captures their workplace mood and tempo. This exercise can provide leaders with a way to talk to their employees about the mood and tempo of the workplace and to get some useful feedback from employees regarding their perceptions of the workplace.

   The approach to this should be fun and upbeat, and any comments on tempo and mood should be appreciated, including songs or lyrics that might be offensive, such as *Take This Job and Shove It.* The leader should respond with a good sense of humor and then ask people to make some constructive suggestions as to what the leader and others may do to improve the workplace melody.

2. You should follow up with the leader to help the leader determine any action steps that might be implemented to improve the workplace culture based on the discussion with the employees.

Emotional Intelligence Exercise 8

Music Clip #1   Describe what it would feel like to work in a place that sounded this way.

_____

_____

_____

_____

Music Clip #2   Describe what it would feel like to work in a place that sounded this way.

_____

_____

_____

_____

Music Clip #3   Describe what it would feel like to work in a place that sounded this way.

_____

_____

_____

_____

Music Clip #4   Describe what it would feel like to work in a place that sounded this way.

_____

_____

_____

_____

Every workplace has a tone. If you listen carefully, you can hear and feel it. It is the rhythm by which people work. If your workplace were music, what kind of music would it be and why? Would it be a joyful waltz or a funeral march? What music is your corporate band playing? What instrument do you play? Are you in tune? In rhythm?

_____

_____

_____

_____

If you could change the tune of your workplace, what would you change it to?

_____

_____

_____

_____

EQ #9

Coming Through

EQ TARGET

✓	**Self-Awareness and Control**
✓	**Empathy**
	Social Expertness
	Personal Influence
	Mastery of Vision

OBJECTIVES

- To help participants acknowledge their emotions in the workplace

- To heighten awareness of the emotions that the leader has during the course of the workday

- To help participants recognize that their emotions impact others in the workplace

- To help participants recognize the appropriate time to express emotions in the workplace and the need for self-control regarding negative emotions.

ESTIMATED TIME

85 minutes

MATERIALS

Emotional Intelligence Exercise #9

RISK/DIFFICULTY

High

COACHING TIPS FOR COACH/TRAINER

Whether emotion should be displayed or kept in check in the workplace depends on many things. The emotionally intelligent leader knows when and how to place some emotions in check. This leader also realizes the impact and harm that negative emotions can have on the workforce.

In addition, the emotionally adept manager also knows when to express emotions related to pride, gratitude, compassion, and caring that positively impact employees. Again this leader realizes the power behind these positive emotions that can serve to motivate and inspire followers.

Therefore, emotion in the leader is neither good nor bad in the workplace. It is how the leader chooses to act on these emotions that has tremendous impact on the overall culture and atmosphere of the work unit. We all know tales of emotionally disruptive bosses who can't seem to hold their temper, who shoot the messenger, and who otherwise intimidate their employees. Many leaders may have worked for bosses of this type and, therefore, may have role models who displayed these characteristics. In other cases, leaders have been taught not to display any emotion, whether good or bad, in the workplace. In these instances they miss the opportunity to express sincere positive feelings that could boost employee morale and contribute to productivity, quality, and creativity.

This exercise is designed to help leaders with the first step to emotional intelligence, which is accurate emotional awareness. Leaders are asked to identify past emotional reactions in the workplace and to identify the results these emotions had on those around them.

TRAINER'S/COACH'S NOTES

	APPROXIMATE TIME

1. Overview

5 minutes

Explain to the group that all leaders have emotion and that the way we express or hold our emotions in check is a critical component of emotional intelligence. Also give examples that support the idea that both expressing emotions and holding emotions in check are both attributes of a good leader. State that emotion in the leader is neither good nor bad in the workplace. But instead, it is being able to distinguish and discern the appropriateness of expressing emotion that characterizes good leaders. "For example, we all know tales of emotionally disruptive bosses who can't seem to hold their temper, who shoot the messenger, and who otherwise intimidate their employees. In other instances, we may also have experienced the power of sincerely expressed positive feelings that boost employee morale and contribute to productivity, quality, and creativity."

2. Objective

1 minute

"The purpose of this exercise is to help you identify some of your emotions that affect the workplace culture. Often as leaders, you block or deny your emotions because somewhere along the line you have learned that it is not appropriate to deal with emotions in the workplace. However, it is much more powerful if you as the leader decide which emotions you should hold in check because they will cause unnecessary damage and when you should express emotions that may have the ability to do good. This puts you, the leader, in control of this very powerful force. The first step in harnessing this power is to recognize the existence of your feelings at work."

3. Give Directions

A. Give the participants Exercise #9.

B. Tell the participants to recall the different emotions that are listed on the handout.

C. Ask participants to focus on two important aspects of each emotion:

    (1) What impact did the emotion have on your behavior?

    (2) What impact did the emotion have on the mood of others in your workplace?

NOTE: Drawing on your own personal experience, give examples to help participants such as:

When I am angry, I get very quiet in the workplace. Normally, I engage in conversation and light-hearted banter, but when I'm angry, all that shuts down.

D. Break participants into groups of four and have them discuss the questions on the worksheet.

40 minutes

4. Debrief in groups of four with the following questions: **40 minutes**

A. What are some of the most common reactions to an angry leader?

B. What are some of the most common reactions to a proud leader?

C. When is it best to keep your emotions in check and not express your emotions to your employees?

D. When can it be useful to express your emotions to your employees?

E. What guidelines would you suggest for displaying negative emotions?

F. What guidelines would you suggest for displaying positive emotions?
List guidelines on a flip chart and discuss with the full group.

Emotional Intelligence Exercise 9

It's important to be aware of the emotions that we experience at work or about work. These emotions often form the backdrop for messages we send to our employees. If we understand our emotions as a leader, we're better equipped to manage the workplace spirit.

Think about the last time you laughed at work. Why? How did it feel? Did others sense your merriment?

_____

_____

Think about a time you felt defeated at work. Did others sense your mood?

_____

_____

When was the last time you were angry at work? Why were you angry? How did it impact your interactions with others?

_____

_____

Think about a time when you were overwhelmed at work. How did it impact the workplace spirit?

_____

_____

Think about a time when you were most proud of your employees/department. How did that pride impact your employees?

_____

_____

Think about a time when you were disappointed at work. What signs might have been visible to your employees?

_____

_____

EQ #10 / Open and Friendly Versus Friendship

EQ #10

EQ TARGET

	Self-Awareness and Control
✓	**Empathy**
✓	**Social Expertness**
	Personal Influence
✓	**Mastery of Vision**

OBJECTIVES

- To help participants develop a sensitivity for developing a caring and open posture with employees

- To help participants define the professional limits of caring in the workplace

- To help participants build bonds but yet not compromise their role as leaders.

ESTIMATED TIME

45 minutes

MATERIALS

Emotional Intelligence Exercise #10

RISK/DIFFICULTY

Medium

COACHING TIPS FOR COACH/TRAINER

Building strong bonds with employees has many advantages for the leader. Most employees also welcome sincere and genuine caring from the leader. The emotionally intelligent leader gains commitment, loyalty, and trust by being able to build sincere bonds with employees. Open communication from employees is critical to remaining competitive and creative in our global world. Therefore, the emotionally intelligent leader understands the need for and importance that must be placed on building sincere bonds with employees.

Sincere bonds are built through both actions and words. Integrity in relationships, honesty in communications, and consistency in actions all produce a workplace atmosphere filled with high trust.

The leader accomplishes this, at least in part, by treating people as equals, by empathizing with their situations, and by acknowledging the sacrifices, skills, gifts, and humanness of each employee.

This exercise encourages leaders to explore the idea of care and support in the workplace. It challenges leaders to define limits for their care and support role in balance with their role as leader.

TRAINER'S/COACH'S NOTES

	APPROXIMATE TIME
1. Overview Explain to the individual or group that the leader's job is easier when the leader is managing in a friendly and open environment. A friendly and open environment allows for free exchange of information, creative ideas flow without fear of criticism, problem solving occurs with greater ease, and a quicker response time to customers or others follow. Also explain that the emotionally intelligent leader knows how to manage the workplace environment sincerely to draw out these characteristics in people. Stress that there is a need for all leaders to answer an important question, "What is the difference between a friendly and open environment and developing a friendship that could jeopardize your role as a leader?"	**5 minutes**
2. Objective "The purpose of this exercise is to help you define what a friendly and open work environment means to you and how best to achieve it in your work environment. This exercise will also ask you to distinguish between a friendly and open environment and a personal friendship."	**1 minute**
3. Give Directions A. Give the participants Exercise #10 B. Ask participants to work individually to complete the worksheet. Ask them to create a personal definition for a friendly and open environment and one for personal friendship. C. Have participants partner to share their personal definitions and philosophies about friendship and a friendly environment. D. Now, ask participants to write an example of how they create a friendly and open environment with employees. Ask participants to consider group strategies versus individual strategies. E. Have participants work in groups of four to share ideas about how to create a friendly and open environment.	**20 minutes**
4. Debrief in the full group. List the suggestions for creating a friendly and open environment with employees. Ask the following questions: (1) How do you know what works and what doesn't? (2) How do individual differences need to be taken into consideration when creating an open and friendly environment? (3) What stops you from demonstrating care and support in the workplace? For example, what messages have you heard that may seem counter to creating strong bonds with employees?	**20 minutes**

Emotional Intelligence Exercise 10

Friendly and Open	Friendship
My definition:	My definition:

Think about each of your employees. Name one thing that you could do to create an open and friendly environment with each employee. Write it down for each employee.

_____

_____

_____

What can you do with your entire work group that would create a more friendly and open environment?

_____

_____

_____

What stops you from creating a friendly and open environment? What messages have we heard that seem counter to creating this type of environment?

_____

_____

_____

EQ #11 — Listening Habits

EQ TARGET

✓	**Self-Awareness and Control**
✓	**Empathy**
✓	**Social Expertness**
	Personal Influence
	Mastery of Vision

OBJECTIVES

- To help participants develop self-awareness related to their ability to listen
- To assist participants in the self-assessment of their listening skills
- To identify negative or disruptive listening patterns that interfere with building good bonds with employees.

ESTIMATED TIME

45 minutes

MATERIALS

Emotional Intelligence Exercise #11

RISK/DIFFICULTY

Medium

COACHING TIPS FOR COACH/TRAINER

The ability to listen attentively and without judgment, advice, or logic is one of the most difficult and most prized skills for leaders to master. Emotionally intelligent leaders know that listening to employees is critical to forming strong bonds and developing an open friendly environment conducive to creativity, productivity, and high quality. They also know that listening reduces conflict and encourages more creative problem solving.

However, negative listening habits can erode the abilities of leaders and diminish their ability to build high trust bonds with employees. Six negative listening habits are often at the root of the inability to listen.

The purpose of this exercise is to identify which, if any of these listening habits, may be interfering with the leader and to heighten awareness of these negative listening habits in the leader's interactions with other people.

The six negative listening patterns are:

1. *The Faker*—All the outward signs are there: nodding, making eye contact, and giving the occasional uh huh. However, the faker isn't concentrating on the speaker. His mind is elsewhere.

2. *The Interrupter*—The interrupter doesn't allow the speaker to finish and doesn't ask clarifying questions or seek more information from the speaker. He's too anxious to speak his words and shows little concern for the speaker.

3. *The Intellectual or Logical Listener*—This person is always trying to interpret what the speaker is saying and why. He is judging the speaker's words and trying to fit them into his logic box. He rarely asks about the underlying feeling or emotion attached to a message.

4. *The Happy Hooker*—The happy hooker uses the speaker's words only as a way to get to his message. When the speaker says something, and frankly, it could be anything, the happy hooker steals the focus and then changes to his own point of view, opinion, story, or facts. Favorite hooker lines are, "Oh, that's nothing, here's what happened to me . . ." "I remember when I was . . ."

5. *The Rebuttal Maker*—This listener only listens long enough to form a rebuttal. His point is to use the speaker's words against him. At his worst, he is argumentative and wants to prove you wrong. At the least, the person always wants to make the speaker see the other point of view.

6. *The Advice Giver*—Giving advice is sometimes helpful; however, at other times, this behavior interferes with good listening, because it does not allow the speaker to fully articulate his feelings or thoughts; it doesn't help the speaker solve his own problems; it prohibits venting; it could also belittle the speaker by minimizing his concern with a quick solution. Well-placed advice is an important function of leadership. However, advice given too quickly and at the wrong time is a turnoff to the speaker.

TRAINER'S/COACH'S NOTES

	APPROXIMATE TIME

1. Overview

2 minutes

Explain to the individual or group that one of the most important skills of the emotionally intelligent leader is his listening skills. Explain that effective listening builds trust bonds and encourages positive problem solving and other behaviors conducive to creativity, quality, and productivity. Tell the group that just like developing a good golf swing, listening takes practice. Explain that it is also helpful to be aware of negative habits that could influence listening skills and work against the mission of building high trust in the workplace.

2. Objective

1 minute

"The purpose of this exercise is to help you gain self-awareness regarding negative listening patterns that may have developed over the years. By being aware of your negative listening patterns, you are then in a position to do something about it. However, listening is second nature to most people, and they don't give it much thought or study. Therefore, sometimes it is very important to step back and analyze your listening habits or to get some input about your listening habits so that you can work to improve them. In this exercise, you will do just that. You will analyze your current listening patterns to determine if you have any negative habits that you would like to break, and you will get some feedback from others on your listening habits."

3. Give Directions

15–20 minutes

A. Give the participants Exercise #11.

B. Review and give examples of the six negative listening habits listed on the worksheet. Demonstrate these negative habits and ask if the participants know of people who practice them.

C. Ask participants to put a check mark next to those negative habits that they think they may sometimes practice with employees.

D. Ask participants to break into groups of five to discuss the impact of each of the negative listening habits on employees. Ask participants to state why these listening habits could cause harm and interfere with building strong bonds with employees.

E. Ask participants to log their listening habits over the next week. Ask them to record any negative listening habits that they practice with employees. Encourage them to actually fill out the form and mark on the form to indicate any negative listening patterns that they have practiced

F. Ask participants the following week to analyze their negative listening habits and make commitments to change negative patterns.

NOTE: Usually this exercise is powerful enough to elicit change on the part of the participant, even if no opportunity for follow up is available.

4. Debrief   **20 minutes**

   A. What patterns did you discover?

   B. Were you more aware of your listening habits? How so?

   C. Were you more aware of the listening habits of others? Please explain.

   D. What changes did you make in your listening habits?

Emotional Intelligence Exercise 11

Empathic listening is fundamental to demonstrating your concern as a leader. Six negative listening habits sometimes prohibit us from being a good listener. Put a check next to the listening habits that you may sometimes practice.

M	T	W	Th	F	
					☐ *The Faker*—All the outward signs are there: nodding, making eye contact, and giving the occasional uh huh. However, the faker isn't concentrating on the speaker. His mind is elsewhere.
					☐ *The Interrupter*—The interrupter doesn't allow the speaker to finish and doesn't ask clarifying questions or seek more information from the speaker. He's too anxious to speak his words and shows little concern for the speaker.
					☐ *The Intellectual or Logical Listener*—This person is always trying to interpret what the speaker is saying and why. He is judging the speaker's words and trying to fit them into his logic box. He rarely asks about the underlying feeling or emotion attached to a message.
					☐ *The happy hooker*—The happy hooker uses the speaker's words only as a way to get to his message. When the speaker says something, and frankly, it could be anything, the happy hooker steals the focus and then changes to his own point of view, opinion, story, or facts. Favorite hooker lines are, "Oh, that's nothing, here's what happened to me . . ." "I remember when I was . . ."
					☐ *The Rebuttal Maker*—This listener only listens long enough to form a rebuttal. His point is to use the speaker's words against him. At his worst, he is argumentative and wants to prove you wrong. At the least, the person always wants to make the speaker see the other point of view.
					☐ *The Advice Giver*—Giving advice is sometimes helpful; however, at other times, this behavior interferes with good listening, because it does not allow the speaker to fully articulate his feelings or thoughts; it doesn't help the speaker solve his own problems; it prohibits venting; it could also belittle the speaker by minimizing his or her concern with a quick solution. Well-placed advice is an important function of leadership. However, advice given too quickly and at the wrong time is a turnoff to the speaker.

EQ #12 / Genuine Listening

EQ TARGET

✓	Self-Awareness and Control
✓	Empathy
✓	Social Expertness
	Personal Influence
	Mastery of Vision

OBJECTIVES

- To help participants develop empathy through improving listening skills
- To improve relationships and bonds with employees by improving our listening skills
- To practice genuine listening skills under stressful conditions.

ESTIMATED TIME

95 minutes

MATERIALS

Flip chart and marker

RISK/DIFFICULTY

Low

COACHING TIPS FOR COACH/TRAINER

Listening skills are central to the emotionally competent leader. However, skill in listening requires far more than technique. True listening requires a mindset that includes the following elements:

- A respectful attitude toward the speaker even when the content of the speaker's message is abrasive

- A open mind willing to hear and seek understanding of the messages of the speaker

- Placing the speaker as an equal and thus worthy of the listener's attention.

These qualities are far beyond technique. Therefore, although the how to's of listening can be taught, unless the mindset is established first, the listening will seem fake or phoney. Leaders must examine not only their technique but also their hearts to truly impact their ability to listen.

Also, listening is far easier when the speaker and the listener have similar values about a particular topic. The most challenging listening occurs when the speaker is saying something in direct opposition to the listener's point of view. In these moments, the emotionally competent leader is able to maintain genuine listening and practice self-control, thus ensuring that the speaker is heard.

The intent of this exercise is to practice both technique and mindset. By developing the skill and the mindset, the leader will forge greater bonds and a more open workplace atmosphere.

TRAINER'S/COACH'S NOTES

	APPROXIMATE TIME

1. Overview
Explain to the individual or group that one of the most important tools for strengthening emotional intelligence is listening. Teach the basic tenets to good listening, including:
  A. Reflective listening to clarify content
  B. Reflective listening to clarify feelings
  C. Listening to nonverbals
NOTE: The trainer or coach should reacquaint the class with the information on listening skills. The trainer or coach should use their judgment to determine how much review is necessary. However, at a minimum, this section should serve as a reminder and review of this important skill.
	20–25 minutes

2. Objective "The purpose of this exercise is to remind you of the importance of developing good listening habits and to practice listening in situations that are challenging." Explain that regardless of your level of expertise, a return to basics is essential when it comes to listening skills.	**1 minute**

3. Give Directions/Part 1
  A. Ask each participant to pick a partner. The instructor should instruct the pairs as follows:
    (1) One person will be the speaker and one will assume the role of listener.
    (2) The speakers will be asked to talk about any subject that they choose. Ask that the speakers choose something about which they feel strongly.
    (3) Instruct the listeners to use listening skills that include asking clarifying questions, reflecting both feeling and content of the speaker's message where appropriate, and practicing appropriate nonverbals. Under no circumstances should the listeners add their own comments or evaluative remarks during the exercise.
    (4) Switch roles after 7 minutes.
  B. Debrief the group with the following questions:
    (1) How did it feel to be listened to?
    (2) Were you tempted as the listener to make comments or tell your own story?
    (3) What was difficult about the exercise?
    (4) What did you learn about your listening habits?
	15 minutes
	
	10 minutes

4. Give Directions/Part 2   **20 minutes**

A. The instructor should prepare some controversial topics and list them on a flip chart. Topics such as gun control, abortion, politics, capital punishment, or other topics that will have supporters on both sides should be selected. Select the first topic for discussion. Ask the group to divide themselves as to pro and con on one of the selected topics. (Ideal group size for one topic is about 10–15. However, it will be important to have supporters on both sides of the argument. If your group is large, you could have several groups going at one time discussing several different topics.)

B. Instruct the group to host a discussion of the topics at hand. Each group can toss a coin to decide which side of the issue goes first. Allow about 20 minutes for discussion.

5. Debrief the full group with the following questions: **25 minutes**

A. At any time did our listening skills erode? What made you think listening was eroding?

B. What caused our listening skills to erode?

C. Did everyone in the group express an opinion? Why or why not?

D. What group dynamics did you observe during the exercise?

E. How does this exercise parallel what can happen in the workplace?

F. What lessons can you learn about your listening skills?

EQ #13 / Tuning in to Our Employees

EQ TARGET

✓	**Self-Awareness and Control**
✓	**Empathy**
✓	**Social Expertness**
	Personal Influence
	Mastery of Vision

OBJECTIVES

- To help participants develop empathy through improving listening skills
- To improve relationships and bonds with employees by improving their listening skills
- To practice genuine listening skills.

ESTIMATED TIME

40 minutes

MATERIALS

Emotional Intelligence Exercise #13

RISK/DIFFICULTY

Medium

COACHING TIPS FOR COACH/TRAINER

Listening skills are central to the emotionally competent leader. However, skill in listening requires far more than technique. True listening requires a mindset that includes the following elements:

- A respectful attitude toward the speaker even when the content of the speaker's message is abrasive

- An open mind willing to hear and seek understanding of the messages of the speaker

- Placing the speaker as an equal and thus worthy of the listener's attention

These qualities are far beyond technique. Therefore, although the how to's of listening can be taught, unless the mindset is established first, the listening will seem fake or phony. Leaders must examine not only their technique but also their hearts to truly impact their ability to listen.

Also, listening is far easier when the speaker and the listener have similar values about a particular topic. The most challenging listening occurs when the speaker is saying something in direct opposition to the listener's point of view. In these moments, the emotionally competent leader is able to maintain genuine listening and practice self-control, thus ensuring that the listener is heard.

The intent of this exercise is to practice listening to employees in the workplace.

TRAINER'S/COACH'S NOTES

	APPROXIMATE TIME

1. Overview

1 minute

Explain to the individual or group that one of the most important tools for strengthening emotional intelligence is listening. Teach the basic tents of good listening, including:

    A. Reflective listening to clarify content

    B. Reflective listening to clarify feelings

    C. Listening to nonverbals

NOTE: The trainer or coach should reacquaint the class with the information on listening skills. The trainer or coach should use their judgment to determine how much review is necessary. However, at a minimum, this section should serve as a reminder and review of this all-important skill.

2. Objective

1 minute

"The purpose of this exercise is to remind you of the importance of developing good listening habits and to practice listening in the workplace with your employees, peers, and others."

3. Give Directions

10 minutes

    A. Give the participants Exercise #13.

    B. Instruct each participant to spend time in the next week practicing listening skills with employees, peers, or others. Ask participants to walk through the department or area, stop, and ask employees how it's going. Then, practice appropriate listening techniques. Remind participants to ask clarifying questions, to be aware of negative listening habits, and to reflect feelings as well as content where appropriate.

    C. Instruct participants to keep a learner's log on this exercise.

4. Debrief the exercise with the following questions:

25 minutes

    A. What did you learn about your listening skills?

    B. What was most difficult?

    C. What was easiest?

    D. Did you learn anything about your employees or the work they were doing? Please elaborate.

    E. Why is listening so important?

    F. Were you tempted to engage in any negative listening habits?

Emotional Intelligence Exercise 13

In practice, next time you walk through your department or area, stop and ask your employees how it's going. Don't have an agenda or specific task for them; just find out what's on their minds. When/if they talk to you, practice genuine listening. Take your time and ask clarifying questions; gain insight into their perspective and feelings about the subject. Be sure to pay attention to your listening skills with employees. Are you engaging in any negative listening patterns? Which ones? What impact do these negative listening patterns have on your employees?

_____

_____

_____

_____

Learner's Log:
Jot down some insights from the above exercise on listening.

_____

_____

_____

_____

_____

_____

_____

_____

_____

_____

EQ #14 / **I Was Appreciated**

EQ TARGET

✓	**Self-Awareness and Control**
	Empathy
✓	**Social Expertness**
✓	**Personal Influence**
	Mastery of Vision

OBJECTIVES

- To help participants develop an understanding of the role that expressed sincere gratitude plays in developing people

- To help participants recognize that genuine expressed gratitude is a leadership skill

- To help participants realize that gratitude can lead to greater cooperation and collaboration between people.

ESTIMATED TIME

45 minutes

MATERIALS

Emotional Intelligence Exercise #14

RISK/DIFFICULTY

Low

COACHING TIPS FOR COACH/TRAINER

One effective way of developing emotional intelligence is to request participants to reflect on situations in their past and draw conclusions about the effectiveness of the methods employed by others. After the reflection, it is important to ask participants to commit to changing their behavior.

Feeling appreciated is a universal need that we have whether in the workplace or in other areas of our lives. When we feel appreciated, predictable positive reactions surface. Yet, in the workplace, our research suggests that 88 percent of the people we interviewed did not feel appreciated.

This exercise is aimed at helping leaders identify the positive reactions in their own experience that surfaced when they felt appreciated. By heightening this sensitivity, leaders will emerge with a greater appreciation of the power behind positive emotions in the workplace such as genuine gratitude. These emotions lead to influence, collaboration, cooperation, and improved productivity.

TRAINER'S/COACH'S NOTES

	APPROXIMATE TIME

1. Overview

Explain to the individual or group that positive emotional energy is contagious, and in the workplace, one of the ways to spread positive emotional energy is through genuine gratitude. Explain that although everyone reacts to gratitude in their own way, when the employee perceives the gratitude as genuine, the reaction is generally positive. Developing an adeptness at using positive influence is central to leadership. Emotionally competent leaders know that they hold tremendous power over the emotional climate of the workplace.

1 minute

2. Purpose

"The purpose of this exercise is to explore your own experiences for evidence of the benefits of feeling appreciated at work. If you think about times when you felt genuinely appreciated for your effort, contribution, skill, or other gifts, you can begin to recognize the power and obligation that you have as a leader. In this exercise, you will recall times when you felt appreciated and also times when you felt unappreciated and discuss the reactions caused by these incidences."

1 minute

3. Give Directions

A. Give the participants Exercise #14.

B. Instruct each participant to complete the worksheet by reflecting on occasions when they felt appreciated by a boss or peer for their efforts. Ask participants to list the occasions on the worksheet and reflect on the feelings that the gratitude caused. Also, ask participants to list times when they felt unappreciated or unacknowledged for some contribution they had made. Again, ask participants to reflect on the feelings caused by this lack of acknowledgment.

15 minutes

4. Debrief

A. In groups of four, have participants answer the following questions:

    (1) What impact does sincere gratitude have on your performance?

    (2) What impact does sincere gratitude have on your self-esteem?

    (3) How can you tell that gratitude is sincere?

B. In the full group, solicit answers from the small groups and list on the flip chart.

C. In groups of four, have participants address the following questions:

    (1) What impact did feeling unacknowledged or unrecognized have on you?

    (2) How can leaders influence others through acknowledgment?

25 minutes

D. In the full group, solicit answers from the small groups and list on the flip chart. Summarize the discussion with the benefits of sincere well-placed gratitude.

Focus the discussion on how the leader can influence and encourage cooperation by bringing out positive emotions in followers.

Emotional Intelligence Exercise 14

As you think about your past work experiences, think about specific examples when a boss expressed sincere gratitude for your work. What impact did it have on you? How exactly did your boss express his or her gratitude? How did you know it was sincere? List those occasions under the header of "champion." Can you recall a time when you did not receive acknowledgment for a job well done? Was there ever a time when others received acknowledgment and you were forgotten? List those occasion under the header of "chump."

Champion—I felt appreciated . . .	Chump—I did not feel appreciated . . .

EQ #15

A Grateful Heart

EQ TARGET

✓	Self-Awareness and Control
	Empathy
✓	Social Expertness
	Personal Influence
	Mastery of Vision

OBJECTIVES

- To help participants recognize the factors that influence their ability to think and assess situations with gratitude

- To encourage leaders to develop a grateful heart, which is conducive to sincere expressed gratitude.

ESTIMATED TIME

40 minutes

MATERIALS

Emotional Intelligence Exercise #15

RISK/DIFFICULTY

Low

COACHING TIPS FOR THE COACH/TRAINER

Sharing positive feelings in the workplace is an emotional intelligence skill that results in a synergistic reaction with employees. Positive feelings create positive energy, and when leaders can focus this energy on the work goals, everyone gains.

However, using positive energy requires many attributes on the part of leaders. The first attribute demands that leaders be genuine about their positive feelings for the people in the workplace and their contributions. If the leader isn't genuine, more harm and damage can be done to try to express feelings that are not honest. The paradox lies in the fact that most leaders have been trained to think critically. Critical thinking allows leaders to make improvements to the status quo, to improve quality, and to otherwise drive for excellence. However, sometimes too much critical thinking has blocked the path to being grateful for the existing contributions, gifts, and skills that are present in the leaders' employees.

Therefore, the challenge for leaders is to maintain their critical thinking, yet balance it with genuine appreciation for what exists. This requires looking at things with a grateful heart and being able to see the good, not just what needs improving in our workplace and in our workforce.

This exercise is aimed at allowing leaders to reflect on how much of their thinking is consumed by critical thinking and how much is rooted in gratitude. As the coach or trainer, you must be sensitive to the fact that critical thinking is a large contributing factor in the success that leaders have. Therefore, acknowledge the power of critical thinking with your participants, yet emphasize the need for balance.

TRAINER'S/COACH'S NOTES

	APPROXIMATE TIME
1. Overview	**2 minutes**

1. Overview

Explain to the individual or group that using positive emotion in the workplace as a means of influence requires sincerely feeling positive about people, their contributions, sacrifices, attitudes, and other gifts that they bring each day to the workplace. Also explain that the best leaders often drive for ways to improve and for excellence, and that that requires critical thinking. Explain the two-edged sword of critical thinking. It is an excellent tool for helping leaders strive for excellence, but on the other hand it can interfere with their ability to spread positive emotion if they are always looking at what's wrong.

2. Purpose   **1 minute**

"The purpose of this exercise is to help you evaluate how much of your thinking is critical and fault finding versus how much of your thinking reflects gratitude. A balance of both is needed to be a good leader; however, critical thinking often outweighs the ability to think positively about people, their contributions, abilities, skills, and gifts. Positive emotion is a powerful force in influencing and developing teams and cooperation in the workplace. Therefore, the emotionally intelligent leader can blend both critical thinking and a grateful heart to come up with the perfect balance."

3. Give Instructions   **10 minutes**

   A. Give participants Exercise #15.

   B. Ask each participant to complete the pie chart on the handout.

   C. Encourage people to think about and honestly reflect on the percentage of time they spend thinking about what's wrong with their workplace and the people in their workplace, versus the percentage of time they spend thinking about what's right with their workplace. Acknowledge the fact that the leaders may indeed be grateful but ask for the percentage of time they think about being grateful.

4. Debrief   **25 minutes**

   A. Break participants into groups of four and ask them to discuss the following:

   (1) What percentage of the time do they engage in critical thinking?

   (2) What percentage of the time do they engage in grateful thinking?

   (3) What message are employees most likely receiving from them?

   (4) How could shifting your thoughts from critical to grateful benefit employees?

   (5) How could shifting your thoughts from critical to grateful benefit the leader?

B. Debrief in the full group. Summarize by stating the benefits to the leader as well as the employee by focusing on positive emotion in the work-place. Explain that this positive emotion is the essence of leadership, influence, cooperation, and building strong bonds with employees.

Emotional Intelligence Exercise 15

Expressing gratitude is important for leaders. However, before you can express gratitude, your thoughts must reflect a grateful heart. Paradoxically, sometimes the reason you're a good leader is because you have trained yourself to think about what's wrong and to look for opportunities for improvement. To that end, you have trained yourself to have a critical heart. Therefore, it's important to assess your heart. In the circle below, create a pie chart reflecting:

■ The percentage of time you think about faults in your employees

■ The percentage of time you think about being grateful for the work your employees perform.

Example:

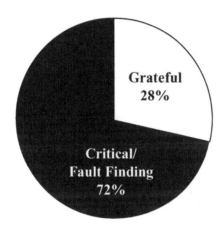

My percentages:

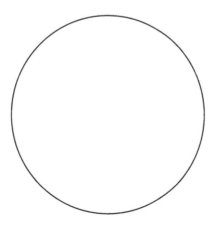

EQ #16 / Gifts

EQ TARGET

	Self-Awareness and Control
	Empathy
✓	**Social Expertness**
✓	**Personal Influence**
	Mastery of Vision

OBJECTIVES

- To help participants recognize the positive attributes of employees

- To help leaders develop a grateful heart, thus enhancing their ability to influence and build bonds

- To help leaders look at the broad array of gifts that are needed for success in the workplace.

ESTIMATED TIME

40 minutes

MATERIALS

Emotional Intelligence Exercise #16

Risk/Difficulty

Low

COACHING TIPS FOR THE COACH/TRAINER

Emotionally intelligent leaders know that it takes a wide range of people to build a successful team. Leaders know that people have different strengths and gifts. The most adept leader knows how to blend everyone's gifts and allow for people's gifts to surface for the good of the task or team. Leaders also know that not all people are alike, and if they expect them to be alike, they'll be quite disappointed. It is the leader who can see and appreciate these differences who has the strongest ability to influence and build a team filled with cooperation and collaboration. This leader is able to bring the gifts forward just when the team needs them and thus enable everyone to succeed.

The emotionally adept leader has the ability to see gifts clearly and to call forth those gifts in the people he or she leads. One important first step is to recognize the gifts that surround the leader. Gifts can be anything from a particular skill a person has, a natural ability that a particular person possesses, a credential, a network, or a personality trait or value that someone in the workplace possesses. Simple things, like someone's sense of humor, might be just what is needed to get through a particularly tough moment. At other times, someone's incredible ability to organize things might just take a project to the next level. So, when leaders think about gifts, encourage them to think in broad terms.

This exercise will help leaders identify specific gifts that their team members possess. It is one of the first steps in being able to tap into the positive emotion that flows from genuine gratitude.

TRAINER'S/COACH'S NOTES

	APPROXIMATE TIME

1. Overview

2 minutes

Explain to the group that all employees have gifts—even the employees who may be most difficult or cause the most headaches probably have things about them that are desirable. Focusing on people's gifts is an important exercise for all leaders. The most emotionally intelligent leaders can quickly see the gifts and strengths in other people. They also find ways to help these gifts surface for the good of the group.

2. Purpose

2 minutes

"The purpose of this exercise is to help you identify the gifts in each of your employees. As leaders you have been trained to think about our employees in terms of their development needs. You ask, 'How could they be better?' There is certainly nothing wrong with developing employees; however, you must balance this quest for development with a genuine appreciation of what is good about your employees. You must ask, 'What special gift, quality, personality trait, character trait, skill, or other quality am I grateful for?' In this exercise, you will discover the gifts that you are grateful for in each of your employees— yes, even your problem employees."

3. Give Directions

20 minutes

A. Give participants Exercise #16.

B. Ask each of the participants to complete the handout by listing the name of each person who works for them to the left of the gift box and then stating some attribute or gift that the employee possesses.

4. Debrief

15 minutes

A. Ask them to pair with another participant to discuss the following:

(1) Did you find this exercise easy or difficult? Why?

(2) Who was the most difficult person to list gifts or attributes for and why?

(3) Who was the easiest person to list gifts or attributes for and why?

B. Debrief in the full group by summarizing the need to think about the gifts that our employees have and genuinely valuing these attributes. Out of this genuineness comes sincere gratitude.

NOTE: You may encounter a leader who has a particular individual for whom she cannot list any positive attributes. If this occurs, discuss the situation with the person after the class. It could be that the employee is a serious problem and the leader is so consumed by the problem that she cannot see beyond these faults. By doing this exercise, we are in no way recommending that seri-

ous problems should be ignored or that leaders should settle for poor performance, just because someone may have a good sense of humor. We are only
asking that leaders try to see a balanced picture of the gifts that people bring
to the workplace. In another section of this manual, we will deal with noncon-
tributors.

Emotional Intelligence Exercise 16

Think about each of your employees as a gift. What do they give to the workplace? Remember to include skills, knowledge, values, or special attributes. List the person's name under the gift box. To the right, list the person's special gifts. These could be something as simple as a sense of humor.

_____ : _____

_____ : _____

_____ : _____

_____ : _____

EQ #17

Yes, But . . .

EQ TARGET

	Self-Awareness and Control
	Empathy
	Social Expertness
	Personal Influence
✓	**Mastery of Vision**

OBJECTIVES

- To help participants determine their commitment to the idea of expressing positive emotions such as gratitude in the workplace

- To help participants determine the benefits of expressed gratitude in their workplaces and also to weigh the risks of such behavior

- To help leaders take the initiative to commit to such actions if they deem it to be useful.

ESTIMATED TIME

45 minutes

MATERIALS

Emotional Intelligence Exercise #17

RISK/DIFFICULTY

Medium

COACHING TIPS FOR THE COACH/TRAINER

Many leaders have been coached or conditioned not to express gratitude or positive emotion in the workplace. Such behavior was considered to lead to employees demanding higher pay raises or raising expectation levels of employees related to career paths, etc. However, the most emotionally competent managers know that genuine gratitude builds bonds and strengthens the trust levels with employees.

The purpose of this exercise is to allow leaders the opportunity to explore the messages they have received regarding the risks associated with expressing positive emotions such as gratitude in the workplace. Leaders will also explore the perceived benefits of expressing such feelings.

TRAINER'S/COACH'S NOTES

	APPROXIMATE TIME
1. Overview Explain to the individual or group that as leaders, we have sometimes received messages that suggest that expressing positive emotions such as gratitude is a mistake because it leads to employees placing demands on leaders. Explain that there are both risks and benefits to expressing emotion and that this exercise will explore both sides of the issue.	**1 minute**
2. Purpose "The purpose of this exercise is to explore both the risks and the benefits of expressing positive emotions such as genuine gratitude in the workplace. This exercise will allow you, the leader, to look at both sides of the issue and decide for yourself whether or not positive emotion is appropriate in your workgroup."	**1 minute**
3. Give Direction A. Give participants Exercise #17. B. Instruct the participants to complete the first two questions on the worksheet.	**15 minutes**
4. Debrief A. Have participants form groups of four to discuss the first two questions on the worksheet. B. In the full group, list reasons on a flip chart for full group discussion. C. Now, ask each participant to complete question 3 privately. D. Debrief by asking for a show of hands of the number of participants who think the risks outweigh the benefits. Ask for elaboration. **NOTE:** Normally, the conclusion is that it is far better to express gratitude in the workplace despite some risks. Occasionally, a strong cultural bias in a particular company may exist against such a practice.	**25 minutes**

Emotional Intelligence Exercise 17

List reasons/risks that make you reluctant to express gratitude.

_____

_____

_____

If your employees think that you genuinely appreciate them, what benefits would you gain?

_____

_____

_____

Do you think the benefits outweigh the risks or vice versa? Draw a balance scale to depict your answer.

_____

_____

_____

EQ #18 / Common Mistakes with Gratitude

EQ TARGET

✓	Self-Awareness and Control
✓	Empathy
	Social Expertness
✓	Personal Influence
	Mastery of Vision

OBJECTIVES

- To help participants distinguish between well-placed genuine expressions of gratitude and using gratitude for the sake of influence

- To heighten participants' awareness of their motivation for expressing gratitude or other positive emotion

- To raise awareness of the feelings created by false gratitude.

ESTIMATED TIME

45 minutes

MATERIALS

Emotional Intelligence Exercise #18

RISK/DIFFICULTY

High

COACHING TIPS FOR THE COACH/TRAINER

Genuine gratitude and other sincere expressions of positive emotion can build bonds with employees, serve as motivation and inspiration for employees, and otherwise improve relations with employees. However, false expressions or expressions done with a motive in mind can cause irreparable harm to our working relationships.

Employees do not like to be manipulated or "played." Employees know when they are being "techniqued" and will resist expressions of positive emotion if they believe the motive is corrupt. Therefore, leaders must make every effort to express positive emotions genuinely with no expectation of gain.

Some of the common mistakes leaders make when "using" gratitude include:

Gratitude for the Sake of Gain

Beware. If leaders use gratitude for gain or manipulation, people will see through them. We repeat: The sole purpose of gratitude is to honor other people by acknowledging their efforts, attitudes, skills, or experience. Yes, we believe there are payoffs from expressing gratitude, but if leaders do this with the payoff in mind rather than the real purpose, the results will be corrupted. People will see it as merely a manipulation tool and will not respond in the same way.

Using Dollars to Measure Gratitude

Leaders also have more to gain if they separate gratitude from monetary rewards. Once they say thank you and here is $100 for your effort, then they begin to judge the effort. It could leave people thinking, "Well, if it was that good, why is it worth only $100, why not $200?" Gratitude isn't about money. It is about truly honoring people's efforts and sacrifices in the workplace with a heartfelt thank you. Fair rewards and compensation surely have a place in an organization, but leaders should think of them separately so as not to contaminate the purity of gratitude. It should be a message from one heart to another. Besides, so many monetary reward programs are formal, lag the effort, and require paperwork and approvals. All of that is contrary to the way gratitude must be delivered.

Blind Gratitude

In addition to pairing gratitude and monetary reward, another mistake can kill the good intentions of gratitude. Sometimes leaders don't see clearly. Perhaps the leader sees that Paolo has done a great job on a project and tells him so. Unfortunately, the leader hasn't seen Phillip's efforts to make the project a success. In an effort to recognize Paolo, the leader could have made Phillip feel hurt or unappreciated.

Redundant Gratitude

Not again please. This leader thanks everyone for everything every minute of the day. The beauty of the words "thank you" is distorted due to overuse. Acknowledgment must be targeted in order for the receiver to gain.

Insincere Gratitude

Don't say thank you if you don't mean it. Employees will know instantly if you are insincere. It's best not to say anything. It will only ruin your credibility if you say things you don't mean.

The bottom line is that the emotionally intelligent leader knows that gratitude or other positive emotional expressions are not to be "used." Instead, they are to be genuine messages that express enthusiasm for and belief in people and their skills, talents, character, and sacrifices. These expressions are not to be done for any motive but simply for truth.

*This list is adapted from *In Search of Honor: Lessons From Workers on How to Build Trust,* by Adele B. Lynn (Belle Vernon, Pa.: BajonHouse Publishing, 1998).

TRAINER'S/COACH'S NOTES

	APPROXIMATE TIME

1. Overview
5 minutes

Explain to the group or individual that emotional intelligence requires honesty in your relationships. When most people think about dishonesty, they think about lying. Certainly, that is one form of dishonesty. But most leaders are not telling blatant untruths. However, well-meaning trainers and instructors have tried to teach managers "techniques" to use to improve performance. These techniques include things like:

- The Sandwich Technique—where you give someone negative feedback sandwiched between positive feedback

- Positive Reinforcement—where managers are told to give positive reinforcement according to specific timetables and for specific gain

- Reward and Recognition Programs—that tie positive feedback to a monetary reward, such as $100 On the Spot Award

Unfortunately, although none of these suggestions are intended to cause mistrust, they often lead to feelings of manipulation or deceit.

2. Purpose
1 minute

"The purpose of this exercise is to examine some of the common mistakes that people make when using gratitude or positive expressions of emotion in the workplace. The hope is that in reviewing these mistakes, you will carefully examine the situations that call for positive emotion and recognize the importance attached to these situations."

3. Give Directions
15 minutes

A. Give the participants Exercise #18.

B. Ask participants to put a check mark next to any gratitude "spirit killers" listed on the following page that they have witnessed. Also, ask participants to reflect on the impact of those spirit killers.

C. Break participants into groups of four to discuss the impact of the gratitude "spirit killers" they have witnessed or experienced in the workplace.

4. Debrief
20 minutes

A. Debrief in the full group by asking the following questions:

(1) Why do you think gratitude is one of those things that can be perceived as manipulative?

(2) When is the risk for the perception of manipulation greatest?

(3) What impact does culture, corporate or otherwise, have on this topic?

NOTE: Cultural influences play a very significant role in the acceptance of expressed positive emotions. Some corporate cultures with little or no trust resist all expressions, even the most sincere, and perceive them as manipulative. Also, in some cultures, the way in which gratitude is expressed is extremely sensitive. Expressions of gratitude in front of peers can be a very negative action in some cultures. In addition, respect for cultural diversity issues is also important. There is no simple answer here, but instead, an obvious caution to leaders is to (a) examine their motives to be sure they are pure, and (b) if pure, use all the emotional intelligence they can muster to determine the best way to express the gratitude.

Emotional Intelligence Exercise 18

Gratitude Spirit Killers—The most common spirit killers and soul suckers related to gratitude are listed below. Put a check mark next to any of the following gratitude spirit killers that you may have witnessed. What do you think is the impact of these spirit killers?

☐ Not enough gratitude

☐ Redundant gratitude

☐ Gratitude for the sake of gain

☐ Insincere gratitude

☐ Blind gratitude

☐ Using dollars to measure gratitude

EQ #19

A Note of Thanks

EQ TARGET

✓	**Self-Awareness and Control**
✓	**Empathy**
✓	**Social Expertness**
✓	**Personal Influence**
	Mastery of Vision

OBJECTIVES

- To help participants develop a habit of expressing heartfelt thanks in the workplace

- To assist participants in thinking in terms of gratitude, especially if they tend to think with a critical eye.

ESTIMATED TIME

50 minutes

MATERIALS

Emotional Intelligence Exercise #19

RISK/DIFFICULTY

High

COACHING TIPS FOR THE COACH/TRAINER

Sometimes, it isn't about lack of emotional intelligence; it's just a matter of habit. Often leaders tell me that they frequently think about things that employees, coworkers, or others have done well, but they forget to tell them that they appreciate their efforts.

Establishing the habit of acknowledging positive emotions is very important. This exercise helps leaders in two ways:

- For those leaders who don't normally think about the good things that people are doing in the workplace, this exercise forces that thought

- For those leaders who think about the good things but fail to acknowledge them, this exercise will encourage action and initiative

Thinking positive thoughts without acting on them is akin to not having the positive thoughts in the first place. Employees can't read the leader's mind, so they may be missing out on important opportunities to touch and inspire people with positive thoughts if they don't bother to express them.

TRAINER'S/COACH'S NOTES

	APPROXIMATE TIME

1. Overview

2 minutes

Explain to the individual or group that habit is an important element that dictates how the leaders are perceived by others. Explain that if leaders are in the habit of never saying good morning, they can be perceived as cold and unfriendly, even if that isn't the truth. Also, explain that habit in expressing or not expressing positive feelings about others is no different. Even though they may greatly value employees or coworkers, if they never express it, they could be perceived as not valuing them.

2. Purpose

1 minute

"The purpose of this exercise is twofold:

- For those leaders who don't normally think about the good things that people are doing in the workplace, this exercise forces that thought.

- For those leaders who think about the good things but fail to acknowledge them, this exercise will encourage action and initiative."

3. Give Direction

5 minutes

A. Give the participants Exercise #19 and a package of 25 thank-you notes.

B. Ask each participant to keep a log for the next week of whom they sent the thank-you notes to and why.

C. Do not set a specific number of notes that the participant must send; however, explain that you will be asking about this exercise at the next session.

4. Follow Up

20 minutes

A. Ask participants to state the number of thank-you notes that they sent during the week.

B. List the number sent on a flip chart in the following categories:
20–25
15–19
10–14
5–9
0–4

5. Debrief

20 minutes

A. Debrief with the following questions:

(1) What do you think constitutes a discrepancy in the number of thank-you notes?

(2) Is there a correct number of notes? Why or why not?

(3) What was the reaction of the people who received the notes?

(4) What other creative nonmonetary expressions would work for you to say thank you to your employees?

Emotional Intelligence Exercise 19

Buy a package of at least 25 thank-you notes. Keep them visible on your desk for two weeks. Every day, look for opportunities to thank people you encounter within your company or organization. You can thank employees, co-workers, even the mail carrier. Just get into the habit of being grateful for people's effort, skills, attitudes, or contributions. Please keep a log of whom you sent a thank-you note and why.

THANK-YOU LOG

Monday

Tuesday

Wednesday

Thursday

Friday

EQ #20

Dumped On

EQ TARGET

	Self-Awareness and Control
✓	**Empathy**
	Social Expertness
	Personal Influence
✓	**Mastery of Vision**

OBJECTIVES

- To help participants develop an understanding of the importance that employees place on fair and equal contributions in the workplace

- To generate an appreciation for leaders who expect fair contributions from all workers

- To understand the role that emotion plays on productivity.

ESTIMATED TIME

50 minutes

MATERIALS

Emotional Intelligence Exercise #20

RISK/DIFFICULTY

Medium

COACHING TIPS FOR THE COACH/TRAINER

In work situations as well as in personal ones, people expect a sense of fairness. When those feelings are violated and people perceive that they are being "used," the result on morale is negative. Therefore, when a legitimately unfair burden is placed on some employees while others are allowed to slide, the resultant environment is negative. To avoid these destructive feelings, leaders must be sensitive to the fact that employees expect the leader to create a work environment that is fair and equal within reason.

Leaders who have a strong sense of emotional intelligence know that part of their role is to manage the contributions in the workplace. They manage the contributions by allowing parties to be held accountable for their share. Leaders who hold *all* people accountable for their share are creating work environments that foster collaboration and cooperation, whereas leaders who allow some people to slide and not perform to their capabilities cause resentment and distrust among peers and among management.

However, leaders know that fairness and perception is a very difficult issue to manage. Employees will always have different perceptions as to what is fair and what is not. However, emotionally intelligent leaders must be sensitive enough to ferret out the genuine concerns from the isolated voice that cries foul for no just cause. These leaders know that the workplace will always provide opportunities for inequity but will work diligently to try to eliminate those inequities within their work unit.

When facilitating this section, you must always work to help the leader balance the legitimate areas for improvement or concerns against a few insatiable complainers. It is important not to dismiss the complainers totally without paying attention to their issues because their issues may contain the kernel of truth needed for the leader to become more effective. Therefore, you should work with the leader to explore all aspects of creating a fair and equal workplace.

TRAINER'S/COACH'S NOTES

	APPROXIMATE TIME

1. Overview

2 minutes

Explain to the individual or group that fair and equal contributions are one of the most common complaints that employees voice in the workplace. Employees are quick to complain about workload, preferred assignments, promotions, or peers who do not contribute on an equal level. Also, explain that these perceptions are often ingrained in a corporate culture and are difficult to change. However, it is the leader's responsibility to create a work environment that has as much fairness as possible. This means that expectations must apply equally, and opportunities must also apply equally. The leader who can create this kind of environment stands to gain in terms of productivity, collaboration, and cooperation from all members of the work team. Feelings of distrust in this area create distrust for the leader, and emotional energy is drained away from the important focus of doing business.

2. Purpose

2 minutes

"The purpose of this exercise is to explore your experiences for evidence of the benefits of being treated fairly in the workplace and for the harm that being treated unfairly in a work situation can cause. Through your own histories, you may be better able to understand the perceptions that your employees harbor. Also, this exercise will help you recognize the negative emotional energy that can be created in an environment that is perceived as unfair. In this exercise, you will recall times when you felt you were expected to carry a fair share of the burden and also times when you felt you were expected to carry an unfair share of the workload and discuss the reactions caused by these incidences."

3. Give Directions

A. Give the participants Exercise #20.

B. Instruct each participant to complete the worksheet by reflecting on occasions when they felt like they participated in an effort where an entire group contributed fairly and equally to the success of the mission. Perhaps the leader served on a team where there was true synergy because the members all pulled together equally. List the occasions on the worksheet and reflect on the feelings that this situation caused. Also, ask participants to list times when they felt they carried an unfair burden of the workload in a particular team or work situation. Again, ask participants to reflect on the feelings caused by this situation. Also, ask participants what if any action the leader took to contribute to either of these situations. Could the leader have done more to equalize the situation in which the participant felt overburdened?

15 minutes

4. Debrief   **30 minutes**

A. In groups of four, have participants answer the following questions:

   (1) What impact does a sense of fair and equal contributions have on the work group?

   (2) What impact does a sense of fair and equal contributions have on your performance?

   (3) How can leaders contribute to this sense of fair and equal contributions?

B. In the full group, solicit answers from the small groups and list on the flip chart.

C. In groups of four, have participants address the following questions:

   (1) What impact did feeling unfairly burdened have on the work group?

   (2) What impact can these feelings cause in performance?

   (3) What actions can leaders take to encourage an environment that is fair and equitable?

D. In the full group, solicit answers from the small groups and list on the flip chart. Focus the discussion on how the leader can influence and encourage cooperation by bringing out positive emotions in followers.

Emotional Intelligence Exercise 20

As you think about your past work experiences, think about specific examples when you felt the workload was fair and equal. Think about times that you knew your boss was in tune with equity issues and took action to equalize the contributions in the workplace. List this information under the heading of champion. On the other hand, when have you felt as if you were in a situation where you were carrying an unfair burden of the work? When have you seen coworkers get away with contributing less, yet suffer little or no consequence? When have you thought the boss was unfairly dumping his or her work on you or your coworkers? What actions did your boss take or fail to take that contributed to unfair contributions? List these under the heading of chump.

Champion— Fair and equal expectations . . .	Chump— Unfair expectations . . .

EQ #21

Doing a Fair Share

EQ TARGET

	Self-Awareness and Control
✓	**Empathy**
	Social Expertness
✓	**Personal Influence**
✓	**Mastery of Vision**

OBJECTIVES

- To help participants assess the level of their employees' contributions in the workplace

- To help participants recognize the emotional impact that lower contributors or slackers have on good employees

- To understand the role the leader has on creating an environment that is perceived as fair.

ESTIMATED TIME

55 minutes

MATERIALS

Emotional Intelligence Exercise #21

RISK/DIFFICULTY

High

COACHING TIPS FOR THE COACH/TRAINER

The level to which people contribute in the workplace is an area that causes concern for the leader as well as peers and coworkers. When workers believe that there is a sense of fair and equal contributions expected by everyone, workers are more accepting of their share. However, when people think that some coworkers are permitted to slack off and not carry their fair share of the work load, resentment sets in. Also, if employees perceive that the boss does not carry her fair share, this also causes a climate of resentment. Needless to say, many of these issues are driven by opinion and perception; however, the emotionally intelligent manager knows that it is her job to manage the perceptions and create an environment that is perceived as fair.

The point of this exercise is to allow participants to honestly evaluate the contribution levels of their employees. Although no two employees' contributions will ever be exactly the same, a general sense of equity within the work team is important. When people in the workplace believe that all are required to do their share, they accept their share more willingly.

When facilitating this activity, coach participants to make judgments based on their overall sense of how well people are contributing. All managers will have some superstars who outperform others. Also, some employees will never be stellar performers. So, despite those normal discrepancies, ask the manager to make her assessments based on a range of what she considers normal performance. Normal performance can be defined as performance that most people can be expected to achieve under normal conditions. For the sake of definition, this is what we mean by a full contributor.

Leaders who have a strong sense of emotional intelligence know that part of their role is to hold people accountable for their share. Leaders who hold *all* people accountable for their share are creating work environments that foster collaboration and cooperation, whereas leaders who allow some people to slide and not perform to their capability cause resentment and distrust among peers and among management.

TRAINER'S/COACH'S NOTES

	APPROXIMATE TIME
1. Overview Explain to the individual or group that it is the leader's role to manage the contributions in the workplace. Explain that although this area will always be one of controversy, a general sense that all people are expected to perform equally is important to high trust climates. Also, explain that when people are not expected to perform their fair share, workers who do perform their share may feel resentful. Also, in many situations, explain that it is the leader who feels resentful when an employee is not performing up to expectations. That resentment can cause further problems and negative emotion in the work group. Remind the group that it is the leader's responsibility to inspire people and that positive emotion is the strongest way to accomplish this. Therefore, a leader who feels resentful is at risk for not being able to bring out the best in others.	**3 minutes**
2. Purpose "The purpose of this exercise is to determine how you evaluate your employees and how you perceive the contribution level of your employees. You will be asked to rate each of your employees against a self-imposed standard called 'full contributor.' A full contributor is a person who performs the full range of the job under normal conditions. The reason for asking you to think about your employees in terms of their contribution to the work team is because it heightens your sensitivity to two issues: (1) your role as the leader to take action with people who are not contributing, and (2) the feelings that slackers cause in others in your work group."	**2 minutes**
3. Give Directions A. Give the participants Exercise #21. B. Instruct each participant to complete the worksheet by reflecting on each employee and determining how that employee measures up to the standard of "full contributor." It is important that managers do not consider a "full contributor" to be their superstar and set the standard of comparison to that level. Instead, a full contributor is the normal level of contribution that you could expect under normal conditions.	**15 minutes**

4. Debrief
A. In groups of four, have participants answer the following questions:
 	
   (1) What impact does a poor contributor have on you, the leader?
 	
   (2) What impact does a poor contributor have on the other contributing members of the work group?
 	
   (3) What responsibility does the leader have to address the poor contributor?
	20 minutes

NOTE: Be sure that the group does not pass off the responsibility of addressing poor performance to other members of the organization, such as human resources, place blame on the union, or otherwise divert the responsibility. If this happens, remind the group of the implications of the word "leader" and sympathize that although it may not be an easy avenue, it is nonetheless the responsibility of the leaders of the organization to set the standards for performance.

B. Ask each person to individually address question 3, 4, and 5. As a trainer or coach, you should make yourself available to the participants for private consultation on these matters. **15 minutes**

Emotional Intelligence Exercise 21

1. On the bar chart below, draw in a bar for each of your employees and one for yourself. Draw the height of the bar relative to the contribution you think each person makes in the workplace. The bar to the left is marked as "full contributor." Draw bars for yourself and your staff relative to that bar.

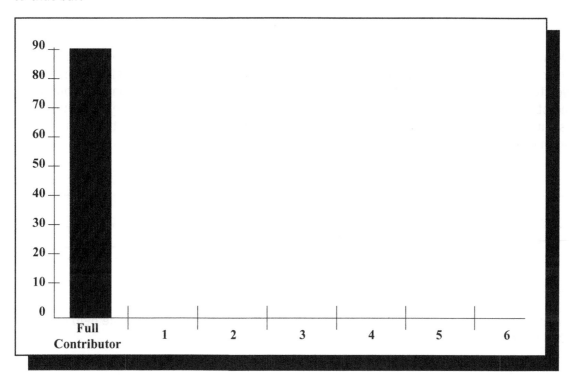

2. Look at the bar chart above. What impact do you think the lower contributors have on you? What impact do you think the lower contributors have on their co-workers?

_____

_____

_____

_____

3. Everyone has an occasional day when they are not contributing at the level they should. However, if the situation occurs frequently, this can cause great resentment in the leader as

well as with coworkers. Are your low contributors on the bar chart above causing serious resentment or anger in you or others? If so, then you must manage the situation by addressing the problems. Is the situation serious enough to impact you or others? Do you think action is needed to address the situation? If yes, answer questions 4 and 5.

_____

_____

_____

_____

4. What actions have you taken to address the lower contributors? Examples of actions could be: discussed and clarified expectations with the employee; held conference(s) with the employee to discuss ways to meet expectations; retrained; discussed the situation with your boss; asked others such as HR for guidance; documented the case; issued disciplinary action; continuously monitored the situation; provided on-going feedback; addressed the situation in the performance appraisal process; or talked to the union steward.

_____

_____

_____

_____

5. What further action do you intend to take? When? If you're unsure, get some help on this. It's too important to ignore.

_____

_____

_____

_____

EQ #22

The Boss's Fair Share

EQ TARGET

✓	**Self-Awareness and Control**
✓	**Empathy**
	Social Expertness
✓	**Personal Influence**
	Mastery of Vision

OBJECTIVES

- To help participants realize that their employees also have expectations for them

- To help participants recognize that sometimes the employee's expectation may cause problems if the employee feels "let down" by the boss's performance

- To understand that communication is critical regarding expectations, whether those expectations are expectations the employee has of the boss or that the boss has of the employee.

ESTIMATED TIME

45 minutes

MATERIALS

Emotional Intelligence Exercise #22

RISK/DIFFICULTY

High

COACHING TIPS FOR THE COACH/TRAINER

This exercise provides some unique opportunities for leaders to look at themselves through the eyes of their employees. The most important point in the exercise for you, the trainer/coach, is to be sure that the right tone is set for doing this.

The exercise asks the leader to evaluate whether or not he is a good leader and contributor *in the eyes of the employees*. Most leaders will probably think they are good contributors; however, the important point in this exercise is whether or not the employee would see them as a good contributor. Why is this important? Because the employee's view in this case may speak to issues, concerns, or expectations that the employee feels the leader is not meeting. Just as leaders become resentful if employees are not meeting their expectations, employees also become resentful if they think the leader is not meeting the expectations of the employees. However, just as we know that sometimes the reason that employees do not meet expectations is due to a lack of understanding of the expectation, the same may be true for the leader. Of course, communication is critical. However, the first step is honest assessment.

So ask your leaders to put themselves in the shoes of their employees and to look at the situation from their eyes. Are employees feeling let down because they can't get answers or resources because the leader is often tied up in meetings? Are employees feeling that they do not have proper resources or training to do their jobs, and do they view that as the leader's responsibility? Or would the employees describe their leader as a full contributor in terms of meeting their expectations?

TRAINER'S/COACH'S NOTES

	APPROXIMATE TIME

1. Overview

Explain to the individual or group that what the leader considers to be significant as far as his contributions to the employee may be different from what the employee thinks the leader should be contributing. Explain that this misperception can cause feelings of resentment in the employee and the employee may believe that the leader is not doing his fair share. Understanding this discrepancy is very important because if left to fester, it could cause problems in the relationships between the leader and the employee. Also, explain that the emotionally intelligent leader understand that misperceptions can cause negative emotions that work against the goals of productivity, creativity, and other factors necessary for success in the workplace. Remind the group that even if the leader is working very hard and doing his job, if the employee thinks that the leader is not, then this is worthy of discussion.

3 minutes

2. Purpose

"The purpose of this exercise is to see your contribution as a leader *from the eyes of your employees.* You will be asked to assess how each employee would rate you according to your contributions to the work team. By understanding how each employee views your contributions to the team, you may be able to uncover some unmet expectations that may help to improve the relationship. Also, this kind of assessment may shed light on where additional communications may be necessary for you and your employees."

2 minutes

3. Give Directions

A. Give the participants Exercise #22.

B. Instruct each participant to complete the worksheet by reflecting on how each employee would rate him or her according to the employee's perception of a "full contributor" boss. Although the leader may not agree with the definition the employee has for "full contributor" boss, the point here is just to determine if there is a discrepancy, not to debate the merit of the employee's opinion.

C. Ask participants to reflect on the reasons that some employees may rate them differently.

15 minutes

4. Debrief

A. Were all the bars on your chart the same size? What do you think contributed to the difference? Have participants, in groups of four, answer the following questions:

   (1) What can/should you do to address the expectations your employees have of you?

25 minutes

(2) Although leaders often spend time learning about the need to address expectations with employees, usually those discussions are one-sided—what the performance expectations are of the employee. What do you think a reversal of this discussion could accomplish? Would it be useful to discuss what employees' expectations of performance are for you?

(3) What responsibility do you have to address this situation?

NOTE: Some groups will immediately recognize the benefit of this type of discussion. However, some leaders will struggle with this concept. Try to focus the discussion on the fact that this is not about employees telling the boss what to do, but rather it is about creating emotionally sensitive and healthy relationships that take into consideration the needs of each party.

Emotional Intelligence Exercise 22

If your staff were asked to draw a bar chart of you compared to a "full contributor" boss, where do you think you would fall? Draw a bar depicting how each staff person would view your contributions. If the level is different, why is it different? Why do you think your staff members would place your level of contribution where they did?

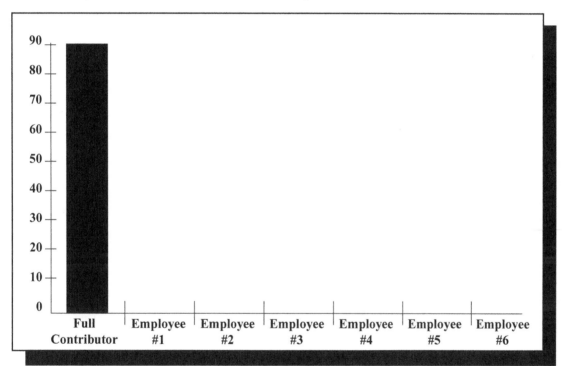

EQ #23

Action/Reaction

EQ TARGET

✓	**Self-Awareness and Control**
✓	**Empathy**
	Social Expertness
✓	**Personal Influence**
	Mastery of Vision

OBJECTIVES

- To help participants realize the impact of their actions on different employees
- To help participants recognize the need for assessing the emotional impact of their actions before taking them
- To help leaders understand the role they have in creating an emotionally positive environment.

ESTIMATED TIME

45 minutes

MATERIALS

Emotional Intelligence Exercise #23

RISK/DIFFICULTY

Medium

COACHING TIPS FOR THE COACH/TRAINER

Newton may not have had emotions in mind when he came up with his third law of motion, which states "For every action there is an equal and opposite reaction." However, this often

applies to human emotion. It is essential for every leader to be sensitive to and assess her actions as to the reaction that they may cause. And unfortunately, unlike the laws of nature, this assessment may have a different answer for each person involved.

However, the emotionally intelligent leader makes conscious choices on how and when she says something or does something because of the reaction that it may cause. To the emotionally intelligent leader, this thought process is almost invisible. Research shows that deliberate thinking about the effect of one's actions on the recipient is a hallmark of intelligence that is most emotional.

This exercise helps to sensitize leaders to the wide range of reactions that one simple action can cause. The intent isn't to determine if the action is appropriate or inappropriate but to realize that many interpretations of the same action may exist depending on who's doing the interpreting.

Encourage leaders to get very creative in their answers. Ask them to have fun and stretch their imagination with this exercise.

TRAINER'S/COACH'S NOTES

	APPROXIMATE TIME

1. Overview

2 minutes

Explain to the individual or group that the more leaders can be sensitive to and predict the reactions to their actions, the better equipped they are to create the work environment they desire. Explain that emotionally astute leaders assess reactions prior to an action and then alter the action based on this assessment. Give personal examples of this kind of assessment, such as deciding not to tell your spouse that you have plans to go golfing for the weekend when she is complaining about how much work there is to do around the house.

2. Purpose

2 minutes

"The purpose of this exercise is to help you stretch your sensitivity to your employees' reactions to your actions. Part of what makes working with people so much fun is that unlike machines, they may have multiple reactions to the same action. The reason that it is important to be able to predict reactions is that you can alter your actions if you think it is appropriate before getting an undesirable reaction."

3. Give Directions

20 minutes

    A. Give the participants Exercise #23.

    B. Instruct each participant to complete the worksheet by reflecting on a few recent memos, e-mails, or verbal communications that she has sent. For each action, ask the leader to imagine the many possible reactions that employees could have. Encourage participants to be creative and have fun with this exercise.

4. Debrief

20 minutes

Have participants, in groups of four, answer the following questions:

    A. Why is it important to give forethought to reactions to your actions as leaders?

    B. What impact could this practice have on creating a desired work culture?

    C. What responsibility do you have to anticipate reactions?

NOTE: Encourage the group to recognize that this is very empowering, not burdensome. The ability to shape a work environment is contingent upon the emotional climate you can create, and this practice is central to creating a desired workplace culture.

Emotional Intelligence Exercise 23

Every action you take or don't take sends a message. Recall the last 10 memos, e-mails, phone calls, or verbal instructions that you sent to any of your employees. In the left hand column jot down the intent of each message. Using your imagination, what messages could someone have gotten that would be different from your intention. Be wild and creative. Think out of the box. Think about how the messages might have made someone feel. Write your answers in the second column.

Ex. Sent memo to remind John about safety meeting.

I don't trust him to remember.

He doesn't have to be responsible for his own calendar.

Safety is important.

I think he is in the early stages of Alzheimer's disease.

I'm being helpful and trying to ease his burden.

EQ #24

Take a Stand

EQ TARGET

	Self-Awareness and Control
	Empathy
	Social Expertness
✓	**Personal Influence**
✓	**Mastery of Vision**

OBJECTIVES

- To help participants realize the importance of commitment toward a goal

- To help participants recognize that commitment toward a goal is a hallmark of leadership

- To help participants understand the damage done by sending mixed messages to employees regarding goals.

ESTIMATED TIME

45 minutes

MATERIALS

Emotional Intelligence Exercise #24

RISK/DIFFICULTY

High

COACHING TIPS FOR THE COACH/TRAINER

Leaders set direction. Leaders decide on what is important for the work team and where the priorities and resources are best allocated. Although the best leaders do this through involvement and influence rather than strong-arm tactics, nonetheless, the leader is the visionary who decides on the path. One common concern of followers is that some leaders do not take a stand when, indeed, it is the leader's responsibility to do so.

Emotionally intelligent leaders recognize that it is important to take a stand. The leader's commitment to the goal leads the way for others to be committed to the goal. When leaders waver, or send mixed messages about the importance of a decided path, followers become confused or even angry. That's not to say that leaders can't change their minds after listening to and engaging their followers. We're talking instead here about leaders who do not give consistent messages about direction and vision and how this can damage bonds and cause followers to question their leader's contribution.

The goal of this exercise is to help leaders examine how important it is for a leader to take a stand. The participants will be asked to recollect occasions when they have committed to follow a certain path and the impact of such a commitment. Leaders will also be asked to examine negative situations when a leader did not stand behind his position.

Sometimes, the leader who lacks self-confidence or self-discipline can take a stand, then back down. This kind of behavior also confuses followers and does not bode well for gaining future commitment from followers.

TRAINER'S/COACH'S NOTES

	APPROXIMATE TIME

1. Overview

2 minutes

Explain to the individual or group that by pure definition, it is the leader's role to be the visionary and decide on the goals and direction of the group. There-fore, the leader's ability to follow through with his commitment to the goal is very important. Sometimes, leaders abandon their commitment or give mixed messages about the desired direction, which confuses or even angers the fol-lowers. Explain that it's not to say that good leaders do not change direction at times, but when the leader is often giving mixed directions, this can cause damage to the bond with followers. Also explain that leadership requires cour-age to stick to commitments that are sometimes unpopular, but, nonetheless, the right course of action.

2. Purpose

1 minute

"The purpose of this exercise is to help you evaluate times in your life when you have taken a stand and remained standing by an issue or goal that you were committed to. Also, you will examine the impact of wavering or changing your direction because you lacked the commitment or courage to stay on course."

3. Give Directions

15 minutes

A. Give the participants Exercise #24.

B. Instruct each participant to complete the worksheet by reflecting on the following:

(1) A time when the participant took a stand on an issue and would not back down, because he believed that it was absolutely the right thing to do.

(2) A time when the participant did not take a stand on an issue and now in retrospect believes that he made a mistake.

(3) A time when the participant took a stand on an issue then didn't commit or follow through.

(4) In each case, ask the participant to reflect on the impact that this had on the followers.

NOTE: The same objective can be accomplished by having participants reflect on the actions of other leaders who took a stand, did not take a stand, or took a stand but then relented. This may be less risky in some groups.

4. Debrief:

25 minutes

A. In groups of four, have participants answer the following questions:

(1) Why is it important for you to take a stand?

(2) How do employees know when you are serious?

(3) What is the impact on followers if you take a stand, then relent when things get tough?

(4) What impact does it have on followers if you do not take a stand when you should?

B. Summarize the following points:

(1) It requires courage to stick to a goal in the face of resistance.

(2) When the followers do not believe that the leader will stick to a path, resistance becomes the norm for the followers.

(3) When the leader has legitimate reasons to change direction, followers understand and respect the decision, provided that the leader usually does not give mixed messages.

Emotional Intelligence Exercise 24

Think about a time when you took a stand on an issue with your staff and persistently followed through. What did you do? How did your staff know that you were serious? How did you feel about this?

_____

_____

_____

_____

_____

Think about a time when you took a stand on an issue and then backed down. How has this impacted your staff? How did it impact you?

_____

_____

_____

_____

_____

Think about a time when you didn't take a stand on an issue and you should have. Why didn't you? How do you feel about that?

_____

_____

_____

_____

_____

EQ #25

I Value, We Value

EQ TARGET

✓	**Self-Awareness and Control**
	Empathy
	Social Expertness
✓	**Personal Influence**
✓	**Mastery of Vision**

OBJECTIVES

- To help participants realize their role in reinforcing and encouraging the workplace values that are operative in their work unit

- To help participants recognize that incongruent values send mixed messages to followers and create confusion or even anger.

ESTIMATED TIME

40 minutes

MATERIALS

Emotional Intelligence Exercise #25

RISK/DIFFICULTY

Medium

COACHING TIPS FOR THE COACH/TRAINER

In addition to setting direction for the work group, leaders also set the values. By values we mean the way in which the work is accomplished. By the actions the leader takes and the words the leader uses, employees get messages about what the leader values. When these messages are consistent, employees know where they stand and what to expect. However, if these messages are inconsistent, followers could be confused. For example, if a leader says that she values customer service, then acts in a way that belittles or demeans the customer's needs, her message and actions could be inconsistent. This kind of inconsistency is based on a conflict of what the leader says she values and what, indeed, the leader values.

Emotionally astute leaders are congruent. They send messages based on their values, and these messages are consistent. Words and actions support one another. This exercise helps leaders evaluate their actions to determine if incongruent messages exist. Of course, no workplace is 100 percent consistent. People understand this and are forgiving if most actions and words work toward a common direction.

Employees are very quick to pick up on values conflicts. They can immediately sense when the leader is sending mixed messages. With strong values, the employee knows which actions are acceptable and which are not. Values set the direction and give the employees guidelines on how they should act.

TRAINER'S/COACH'S NOTES

	APPROXIMATE TIME

1. Overview

Explain to the individual or group that values set the tone in the workplace for how the work is to be done. Values help decide the difficult choices. Values form the basis for those choices. However, when the values are inconsistent, the followers become confused or even angry. The emotionally intelligent leader knows that in order to be a leader and to influence and bond with followers, she must set the values and let the group know what those values are—both by word and by deed. The emotionally intelligent leader also knows the damage done by actions and words that are contrary to those values.

2 minutes

2. Purpose

"The purpose of this exercise is to help you evaluate the values that are important to you and the values messages that you send to your employees. Sometimes, these messages can be incongruent, and that can damage the integrity of your relationships with your employees. In addition, when the values messages are clearly understood, the leader's job is easier because employees have a basis from which to work."

2 minutes

3. Give Directions

A. Give the participants Exercise #25.

B. Instruct each participant to complete the worksheet by marking with a different color ink the following:

(1) The five values that the leader thinks are most important to the work unit.

(2) The five values that the employees believe are most important to the work unit.

(3) The five values that the company believes are most important.

(4) Examine the sheet for inconsistencies.

10 minutes

4. Debrief:

A. Have participants, in groups of four, answer the following questions:

(1) Did you discover any inconsistencies in what you value, what employees think you value, and what the company values? Please elaborate.

(2) Why is it important for leaders to set the values that are most important in their work unit?

(3) What happens when the values that you say you value and the values that the organization values are different?

(4) What impact do inconsistent values have on the work unit?

25 minutes

(5) How can you reinforce the values that you would like to implant in the workplace?

B. Summarize the following points:

(1) ALL groups have values. The values that will prevail with be the values that are most often reinforced.

(2) If the leader doesn't set the values, someone else will. If left to chance, the values that emerge may not be the most desirable values for the work group.

(3) The leader has tremendous power in determining the values, but in order for the values to "stick," all actions, words, and reinforcement must support the desired values.

Emotional Intelligence Exercise 25

Below is a list of values that could be present in the workplace. Circle the five values with a blue ink pen that you truly value most in your work unit. Be careful not to circle what you say you value or the company says you should value, but instead circle what you truly value. Feel free to add to the list. With another color ink, circle the five values you think your employees believe are most important to you. Where are the discrepancies?

Lightning Speed   Perfection
Harmony   Beauty
Respect   Truth
Cleanliness   Order
Safety   Open-Mindedness
Customer Satisfaction   Straightforwardness
Responsibility   Resourcefulness
Creativity   Sense of Community
Entrepreneurship   Independence
Team Attitude   Helping Others

_____   _____

_____   _____

_____   _____

_____   _____

Using the list above, circle the five values you think your company or organization values most. (If your company has stated values, these may or may not be congruent with what you think the organization values most.) Any discrepancies?

EQ #26

Contribution Spirit Killers

EQ TARGET

✓	**Self-Awareness and Control**
✓	**Empathy**
	Social Expertness
✓	**Personal Influence**
	Mastery of Vision

OBJECTIVES

- To help participants identify the known "spirit killers" in the workplace

- To help participants recognize that these "spirit killers" can create negative workplace cultures

- To help leaders recognize "spirit killers" in their own behavior.

ESTIMATED TIME

45 minutes

MATERIALS

Emotional Intelligence Exercise #26

RISK/DIFFICULTY

High

COACHING TIPS FOR THE COACH/TRAINER

Based on our research, employees identified four "spirit killers" that they believe contribute to low productivity and morale. These four spirit killers are:

1. Expectations that apply only to some—Employees feel betrayed when leaders expect some employees to perform at a given level while they perceive that other employees are not held to the same standard. When this occurs, some employees react by withholding their efforts. Not all employees withhold their contributions, but even with those who continue to perform, resentment builds against coworkers and the leader. Employees perceive that it is the leader's responsibility to uphold the standards fairly, so when this does not occur, they blame the leader for not doing his job.

2. Incongruent actions—When the boss does or says one thing and then turns around and does or reinforces the opposite, employees are quick to see the inconsistencies. High trust environments are built on consistent and congruent actions. Therefore, when actions and words are too often perceived as inconsistent, trust erodes. This erosion of trust dampers morale and creates negative emotion inconsistent with high productivity.

3. Wimpy leaders—When leaders are perceived as not taking a stand on issues that require a decision, employees get discouraged. The employees' perception is that when a decision is clearly the responsibility of the leader, the leader should make the decision. Indecision drains energy and breaks up the positive flow of energy, thus destroying momentum. (We are not suggesting that employees want leaders to make all decisions. Participative decision making is preferred in many situations by both employees and leaders. However, at times, participative decision making is not the right choice, and at those times, leaders need to step up to the plate and make the decision.)

4. No follow-through—When the leader takes a stand and doesn't follow through with the expectation, employees learn that the leader's words have no meaning. The leader creates a culture where employees know that if they wait long enough, nothing will happen because the leader won't follow through. This is demoralizing for employees and breaks trust bonds because the words that the leader speaks are not backed by actions.

This list was adapted from *In Search of Honor: Lessons From Workers on How to Build Trust,* by Adele B. Lynn (Belle Vernon, Pa.: BajonHouse Publishing, 1998).

Emotionally intelligent leaders know that the spirit killers listed above come with a price. That price includes low morale and a drain of energy. In order for a leader to accomplish something, he or she must be able to muster positive evergy toward a goal. The actions listed above kill that force and make goals much more difficult to achieve.

TRAINER'S/COACH'S NOTES

	APPROXIMATE TIME
1. Overview Explain to the individual or group that the leader has to be careful of four spirit killers that sometimes invade the workplace. Explain the four spirit killers listed above to the group. Give examples of these spirit killers from your own work experience. Explain that emotionally intelligent leaders know that these spirit killers come with a price. That price includes low morale and a drain of energy. In order for a leader to accomplish something, he must be able to muster positive energy toward a goal. The actions listed above kill that force and make goals much more difficult to achieve.	**5 minutes**
2. Purpose "The purpose of this exercise is to help you identify the spirit killers in your workplace and to come up with suggestions to help eliminate them."	**1 minute**

3. Give Directions
 	
  A. Give the participants Exercise #26.
 	
  B. Instruct each participant to complete the worksheet by thinking about the spirit killers that may be at play in the workplace.
 	
  C. Ask participants to come up with specific items that may be contributing to these spirit killers.
 	
  D. Ask participants to devise ways to eradicate these spirit killers.
	15 minutes

4. Debrief
 	
  A. In groups of four, have participants answer the following questions:
 	
    (1) Which spirit killers exist in your workplace?
 	
    (2) Why is it important for leaders to be aware of these spirit killers?
 	
    (3) What damage can these spirit killers have on employee morale?
 	
    (4) How can you eradicate these spirit killers?
 	
  B. Summarize the following points:
 	
    (1) All groups will experience these spirit killers at some time. It is when the spirit killers occur more frequently than not, that permanent harm is done to the culture.
 	
    (2) Groups are forgiving when these actions occur occasionally; however, the integrity of the leader can be harmed if they occur too frequently.
	25 minutes

Emotional Intelligence Exercise 26

Spirit Killers and Soul Suckers—Four of the most common spirit killers related to contributions and expectations in the workplace are listed below. Which spirit killers do you think may be affecting your workplace? Put a check mark next to those items. Why is it important for leaders to be aware of these spirit killers? What damage can these spirit killers have on employee morale? How can you eradicate these spirit killers?

☐ Expectations that apply only to some

☐ Incongruent actions

☐ Wimpy leaders

☐ No follow-through

EQ #27 / You Expect Me to What?

EQ TARGET

✓	**Self-Awareness and Control**
✓	**Empathy**
	Social Expertness
✓	**Personal Influence**
	Mastery of Vision

OBJECTIVES

- To help participants identify the expectations employees have of them in the workplace

- To help participants recognize that these expectations are important to the employees and that living up to the employees' expectations builds bonds of trust

- To help leaders recognize that open communication is critical for high trust relationships.

ESTIMATED TIME

40 minutes

MATERIALS

Emotional Intelligence Exercise #27

RISK/DIFFICULTY

High

COACHING TIPS FOR THE COACH/TRAINER

The worker/leader relationship is filled with expectations. Most leaders have been given instruction on how to set expectations with employees. However, very seldom has the leader been given much assistance on soliciting expectations from employees. Therefore, often, employees feel that the relationship is one sided. And in reality, it is; the employees are hired to do a job, and if they don't do it, the company has no need for them.

However, the emotionally intelligent leader recognizes that she has much to gain by being an equal participant in the relationship. Equal participation, however, means that not only does the leader have expectations that she can set for the employees, but that the leader must be open to expectations that the employees have for the leader. These expectations should be discussed up front and be open for evaluation. (The fact of the matter is that employees have expectations of the leader regardless of whether or not the leader is aware of the expectations. The emotionally astute leader simply knows that it is better if she knows what those expectations are.)

TRAINER'S/COACH'S NOTES

	APPROXIMATE TIME

1. Overview

2 minutes

Explain to the individual or group that feedback from employees is one of the most powerful tools the leader can receive. Also explain that in most human relationships, there are expectations. Those expectations are particularly strong in the employee/leader relationship. Also, the expectations go beyond the obvious expectations of a good day's work for a good day's wage. The leader can tap into tremendous power when she is sensitive to the expectations of employees and can work to meet expectations that support the common workplace goals.

2. Purpose

1 minute

"The purpose of this exercise is to help you identify the expectations that employees have of you. You will do that by asking employees for feedback. By understanding your employees' expectations, you will be better equipped to serve your team and reach your goals."

3. Give Directions

15 minutes

A. Give the participants Exercise #27.

B. Instruct each participant to talk to each of her employees to determine their expectations regarding contributions in the workplace. Coach participants to listen carefully. If some of the employees' expectations are different from what the leader expects, instruct the leader to write them down and meet with the employees later to discuss why the expectations are not reasonable or possible for the leader to consider.

C. Ask participants to come up with specific action items based on their interviews with their employees.

4. Debrief:

20 minutes

After the interviews, schedule some time with the participants individually to discuss the following:

A. What about your meetings with your employees surprised you?

B. What about your meetings with your employees could you have predicted?

C. Based on your discussions with your employees, do you anticipate any changes in your actions as the leader? If so, what?

Emotional Intelligence Exercise 27

In practice, nothing can substitute for good communications. Talk to each of your employees about contributions and expectations in the workplace. Ask them the following questions:

1. What do you expect from me that I don't always provide for you?

2. Tell me about a time when you were disappointed and felt that I could have taken a different action from the action I took.

3. What is your opinion about the distribution of the workload in our department?

4. How would you distribute the workload differently?

5. What do I do that sometimes causes confusion or sends mixed messages?

EQ #28 Great Vision

EQ TARGET

✓	**Self-Awareness and Control**
	Empathy
	Social Expertness
✓	**Personal Influence**
✓	**Mastery of Vision**

OBJECTIVES

- To help participants develop an understanding of the qualities associated with great vision

- To help participants determine or assess these qualities against their own strengths in this area

- To help participants determine how vision affects their role as a leader.

ESTIMATED TIME

50 minutes

MATERIALS

Emotional Intelligence Exercise #28

Biographical reading material of a great leader selected and admired by the participant. Suggestions are included in the resource listing at the end of the book.

RISK/DIFFICULTY

Low

COACHING TIPS FOR THE COACH/TRAINER

Vision serves two essential purposes for the leader. A clear vision helps the leader to stay motivated toward his work. The clearer the leader can see the mission, the better chance the leader has to achieve it. In addition, the leader with a clear vision is better equipped to interact with and inspire followers. It's just not OK for a leader to be wishy-washy about what he intends to accomplish. The term "leader" implies that you have a mission or a cause, and the vision is essential if the leader is to engage himself and his followers in a clear direction.

The purpose of this exercise is to help leaders discover for themselves the power that vision has. By studying some great leaders, the participants can answer essential questions related to the vision of these leaders and determine how that vision impacted the leader's ability to achieve.

The participants should be allowed to select leaders they most admire. This works especially well if you are coaching an individual leader. However, if you are using this exercise in a group setting, you may assign specific readings for the full group.

TRAINER'S/COACH'S NOTES

	APPROXIMATE TIME

1. Overview

2 minutes

Explain to the individual or group that one of the most distinctive hallmarks of leadership is vision. A clear vision enables both leader and follower to understand how the mission is to be lived. Great leaders are motivated by their mission and vision. It is vision that serves as the way to inspire others toward the mission. If a leader does not have or cannot clearly articulate his vision, followers will not be inspired to follow. Also explain that if people examine great leaders of the past, one common link is that all great leaders have a mission and a clear vision of how that mission will be achieved.

For example, Martin Luther King, Jr.'s vision was to nonviolently create opportunities and equality for people of color. Franklin D. Roosevelt's vision was to get Americans back to work and move the country out of the Great Depression. Fred Smith of Federal Express had the vision to deliver packages anywhere in the United States overnight. And Herb Kelleher, CEO of Southwest Airlines, wanted to have fun and make a profit.

2. Purpose

1 minute

"The purpose of this exercise is to explore great leaders and their vision to determine the impact that vision had on their success. Also, as you explore great leaders, you will identify the characteristics and qualities regarding vision that these leaders exhibited. Lastly, you'll compare your own qualities related to the vision of these great leaders. In doing this, you will come to identify your own strengths and weaknesses related to vision."

3. Give Directions

20 minutes

A. Give the participants Exercise #28.

B. If you expect all participants to read the same material, instruct them on the selection that you would like for them to read. If you are permitting each of the participants to select their own piece from a reading list, ask them to inform you of their selection.

C. Instruct each participant to read the selection and complete the worksheet by analyzing and listing the leader's characteristics or qualities related to vision. These qualities are usually items such as passion, perseverance, persistence, focus, and unwavering motivation.

D. Ask each participant to rate themselves on a scale of 1 to 10 on the qualities that they selected.

4. Debrief

25 minutes

Ask participants in groups of four to answer the following questions:

A. What are the qualities related to vision that great leaders exhibit?

B. In the face of adversity or criticism, what usually happens to the great leader's vision/mission?

C. What can you learn about great leaders and the connection to vision?

D. How do you rate yourself on the qualities of vision? Where would you like to improve?

Emotional Intelligence Exercise 28

Think about a leader who has or had great vision and clearly and cleverly articulated it. Some examples might be:

- Martin Luther King, Jr., whose vision was to nonviolently create opportunities and equality for people of color.

- Franklin D. Roosevelt, whose vision was to put the people of America back to work and move the country out of the Great Depression.

- Fred Smith of Federal Express, whose vision was to deliver packages anywhere in the United States overnight.

- Herb Kelleher, CEO of Southwest Airlines, whose vision of having fun and making a profit placed Southwest Airlines at the top of the heap.

When you think of a leader who had or has great vision, what qualities come to mind? List words that describe leaders with great vision. Generally, words that come to mind are listed below. Mark an "x" on the scale to indicate your strengths relative to the following. (One is low, ten is high.)

Passion

| 1 | 2 | 3 | 4 | 5 | 6 | 7 | 8 | 9 | 10 |

Perseverance

| 1 | 2 | 3 | 4 | 5 | 6 | 7 | 8 | 9 | 10 |

Persistence

| 1 | 2 | 3 | 4 | 5 | 6 | 7 | 8 | 9 | 10 |

Focus

| 1 | 2 | 3 | 4 | 5 | 6 | 7 | 8 | 9 | 10 |

Unwavering Motivation

| 1 | 2 | 3 | 4 | 5 | 6 | 7 | 8 | 9 | 10 |

EQ #29

My Vision

EQ TARGET

	Self-Awareness and Control
	Empathy
✓	Social Expertness
✓	Personal Influence
✓	Mastery of Vision

OBJECTIVES

- To help participants develop or refine their vision for their workplace unit or department
- To help participants use words or phrases to connect their thoughts to their vision.

ESTIMATED TIME

30 minutes

MATERIALS

Emotional Intelligence Exercise #29

RISK/DIFFICULTY

Medium

COACHING TIPS FOR THE COACH/TRAINER

All levels of leaders must have a vision for their area, department, or company. This exercise is aimed at helping leaders to conceptualize their vision or refine an existing one.

It is important to differentiate the company vision statement from the vision that leaders have for their areas. Although the vision of the leader should support and feed into the larger company vision, it is certainly appropriate for each leader to have a "vision within the vision." This enables leaders to personalize their work and inspire their followers to "see" how their unit or department fits into the larger picture.

As a coach for this exercise, it is important that you ask participants to stay focused on their company's mission/vision during this exercise. Yet, many leaders need encouragement to realize that they must also bring the company's vision into the area that they manage—regardless of whether that area comprises two people or two thousand people.

Sometimes people who are leading very small groups or units feel that they have no authority or power to have their own vision. Explain that they have a vision whether they think about it or not. Also, explain that their vision is somehow communicated to employees. For example, their vision may be that they lead a small powerless unit that makes no difference to the company. Sure enough, followers will pick up on the vision, and it may not be the message that is intended.

TRAINER'S/COACH'S NOTES

	APPROXIMATE TIME
1. Overview Explain to the individual or group that all leaders must have a vision. When working within a company, leaders who are somewhere in the middle must be sure that their vision fits with the company mission/vision; however, each leader must have a vision. Sometimes people who are leading very small groups or units feel that they have no authority or power to have their own vision. Explain that they have a vision whether they think about it or not. Also, explain that their vision is somehow communicated to employees. For example, their vision may be that they lead a small powerless unit that makes no difference to the company. Sure enough, followers will pick up on the vision, and it may not be the message that is intended. Also explain the power that vision plays for great leaders and their followers. Draw on information from EQ 28 for this explanation.	**1 minute**
2. Purpose "The purpose of this exercise is to help you discover or redefine your vision for your department or area. As a leader, your vision will be one of the strongest tools that you have to influence and inspire followers in a given direction. The vision allows followers to 'see' the direction where you intend to lead them."	**1 minute**
3. Give Directions A. Give the participants Exercise #29. B. Instruct each participant to complete the worksheet by reflecting on each of the components listed and then listing words or phrases that come to mind when the participant "sees" the perfect future. For example, for the component labeled "people," the leader's vision may be that people are perfectly trained and cross trained, and all exhibit excellent team player attributes. C. Coach participants to list the most important words or phrases that describe their vision for each element on the worksheet.	**15 minutes**
4. Debrief by asking the following questions: A. How do your words or phrases stray from your company's vision? B. How do your words or phrases support your company's vision? **NOTE:** If the participant's words or phrases differ from or are contradictory to the company's vision, encourage participants to discuss these differences with you privately to identify a plan of action.	**15 minutes**

Emotional Intelligence Exercise 29

Imagine your department or area in the next few years. Ideally, what do you want to see?

Consider people, product, customers, equipment, machinery, technology. Imagine each of these elements. Create a vision of the future for your area. List words or phrases that come to mind.

People

Product

Customers

Equipment/Machinery

Systems/Technology

EQ #30

Inspiring Words

EQ TARGET

	Self-Awareness and Control
	Empathy
	Social Expertness
✓	Personal Influence
✓	Mastery of Vision

OBJECTIVES

- To help participants create words that inspire their followers and connect them to the leader's vision

- To help participants recognize the power of words in connecting followers to the leader's vision

- To elevate the significance of words as a tool for leaders to use for inspiring followers.

ESTIMATED TIME

40 minutes

MATERIALS

Emotional Intelligence Exercise #30

RISK/DIFFICULTY

High

COACHING TIPS FOR THE COACH/TRAINER

The purpose of this exercise is to challenge any leader who holds to the notion that actions speak louder than words to at least consider the inspiring quality of well-chosen words and the impact these words can have on followers. Also, this exercise will assist leaders in selecting inspiring words that articulate their vision to their employees.

Words engage the heart and the imagination. The words leaders use to communicate their mission/vision can transform the message from one that is boring and mundane to one that is meaningful and worthy. Consider the following examples:

Uninspiring	Inspiring
To give presentations	To give moving presentations to business executives in a beautiful, comfortable nature- and park-like setting where great learning is inspired.
To produce comfortable chairs	To produce chairs that transform tired and achy bodies into refreshed souls who feel capable of conquering the world.
To design stores	To design stores that irresistibly draw attention, peak curiosity, create the illusion of mystery, and are luxurious to the eyes.

You may wish to have examples of the spoken word that have inspired followers to act. Of course, words must be backed by action. So, as the coach, be careful not to overplay the importance of words over actions. Both are important to inspire followers to action. You should communicate that leaders must have both consistent actions and words in order to be truly inspiring.

TRAINER'S/COACH'S NOTES

	APPROXIMATE TIME

1. Overview

Explain to the individual or group that leaders must be able to articulate their vision in a way that engages the followers. Words are the vehicle for articulating vision, and therefore, the leader should select words carefully and craft them for the desired emotional connection to the vision. Give the examples listed in the coach's notes to distinguish between uninspiring and inspiring words. Explain that words are as important as actions to fully engage the follower. Explain that words are often the first encounter with the leader's vision; therefore, words are incredibly important. Ask the group to consider how words impacted the hearts of followers in the following cases: Martin Luther King, Jr.'s inspiring "I have a dream" words; John F. Kennedy's call to action "Ask not what your country can do for you;" and Abraham Lincoln's reflective "Four score and seven years ago." Use these examples to support your point that words are significant.

NOTE: Do not attempt to make the point that words are the most significant aspect of leadership but instead explain that they play a very supportive role in driving one's vision.

2 minutes

2. Purpose

"The purpose of this exercise is to help you select words that communicate your vision to your employees in an inspiring way. Selecting words that capture exactly your vision is a way to clarify your own thinking about your vision as well as give people a consistent message about what is important."

1 minute

3. Give Directions

A. Give the participants Exercise #30.

B. Instruct participants to complete the worksheet by reflecting on the words and phases they selected in EQ #29. These words and phrases captured their vision related to people, products, customers, equipment, technology, etc.

C. For each of the words or phases selected in EQ #29, have participants rewrite the words to capture a more emotional involvement with the vision. For example, an automotive leader wrote that he wanted his people to be team players; he rewrote the phrase "team players" as "Super Bowl contenders who dress to win each day."

D. Encourage participants to get creative with language and to write using "word pictures."

20 minutes

4. Debrief by having the participants in groups of four answer the following questions:

A. What impact do boring words have on followers?

B. How can word pictures serve to inspire followers?

20 minutes

Emotional Intelligence Exercise 30

Leaders with consistent, repetitive, and inspiring messages are most successful in communicating. Inspiring words are words that engage the heart and the imagination. Consider the difference in the following examples:

Uninspiring	Inspiring
To give presentations	To give moving presentations to business executives in a beautiful, comfortable nature- and park-like setting where great learning is inspired.
To produce comfortable chairs	To produce chairs that transform tired and achy bodies into refreshed souls who feel capable of conquering the world.
To design stores	To design stores that irresistibly draw attention, peak curiosity, create the illusion of mystery, and are luxurious to the eyes.

Look at the phrases you created in EQ #29. Rewrite them using more inspiring words.

EQ #31

Sharing Your Vision

EQ TARGET

	Self-Awareness and Control
	Empathy
	Social Expertness
✓	Personal Influence
✓	Mastery of Vision

OBJECTIVES

■ To help participants realize the importance of sharing their vision with those with whom they interact

■ To help participants realize that vision must be communicated often to have the most impact.

ESTIMATED TIME

45 minutes

MATERIALS

Emotional Intelligence Exercise #31

RISK/DIFFICULTY

Medium

COACHING TIPS FOR THE COACH/TRAINER

The idea of having a vision and not sharing it with employees and others in the organization is fruitless. For vision to take hold, the leader must share it often and do so passionately.

This exercise will assess whether or not participants have shared their vision with people within the organization. If they have shared their vision, your job as the coach is to reinforce the need to share the vision continually. If the participants have not shared their vision frequently or with many levels in the organization, your job is to encourage the participants to do so.

The following reasons support the need to share the vision:

1. Followers are not mind readers. The leader cannot expect others to share the mission/vision unless it is stated.

2. Sharing the vision reinforces the way in which the leader perceives the ideal future.

3. Sharing the ideal future puts all members of the team on the same path.

4. Sharing the ideal future allows people to bring creative energy and purpose to the vision.

5. Sharing the ideal allows others in the organization to see the direction in which the leader is headed.

The leader's job is to tie everyone's actions and thoughts to the vision every day.

TRAINER'S/COACH'S NOTES

	APPROXIMATE TIME
1. Overview Explain to the individual or group that vision is essential because of the reasons listed in the coach's notes. Explain that without vision, people have no way of knowing what the leader wants or what direction the leader is taking.	**2 minutes**
2. Purpose "The purpose of this exercise is to help you assess the degree to which you have shared your vision with people in your organization."	**1 minute**

3. Give Directions
  A. Give the participants Exercise # 31.
  B. Instruct each participant to complete the worksheet by reflecting on the questions listed. Ask participants to explore the degree to which their boss, their employees, and their peers are aware and can articulate the participant's vision. Coach participants that often as leaders, they may think they have stated their vision and perhaps they have on occasion, but the true question to ponder is "Are others really aware of your vision for your unit or department?"
  C. State that as leaders, one of their primary responsibilities is to keep people focused on the vision. This vision should include elements such as how people are expected to work together as a team; how customers are to be served; how equipment and technology fare in the work. Instruct the group to answer question #5 regarding how often they talk about their vision with these elements in mind.
	15 minutes

4. Debrief the group by asking the following questions:
  A. Does anyone feel that you must go back and discuss your vision with the boss? Why? Why not?
  B. Does anyone feel that you must go back and discuss your vision with employees? Why? Why not?
  C. Does anyone feel that you must go back and discuss your vision with peers? Why? Why not?
  D. Does anyone feel that your mission does not fit into the larger vision of your company?
NOTE: Summarize this discussion with the point that the leader's job is to constantly—at least daily—reinforce the vision with employees.
	25 minutes

Emotional Intelligence Exercise 31

1. Have you shared your vision with your boss?

   _____ yes   _____ no

2. If you are a leader in the middle, does your vision fit in with the larger vision of your company? Board of directors?

   _____ yes   _____ no

3. Have you shared your vision with your employees?

   _____ yes   _____ no

4. How often do you talk about your vision? Place a check mark next to the appropriate response.

   _____ Once an hour

   _____ Once a day

   _____ Once a week

   _____ Once a month

   _____ Once a year

If your answer is less than once a day, you are not communicating your vision enough. Every action you take and every word you speak should reinforce your vision. Your job as the leader is to tie everyone else's actions and thoughts to the vision.

EQ #32

Who Invents?

EQ TARGET

✓	**Self-Awareness and Control**
	Empathy
	Social Expertness
✓	**Personal Influence**
	Mastery of Vision

OBJECTIVES

- To help participants realize the need to invite employees to join in the vision

- To help participants recognize that they may dominate the vision and, therefore, cause the employees not to engage in the work.

ESTIMATED TIME

35 minutes

MATERIALS

Emotional Intelligence Exercise #32

RISK/DIFFICULTY

High

COACHING TIPS FOR COACH/TRAINER

Vision is an important hallmark of leadership. However, it is essential that the leader share the vision with her employees. Sharing the vision allows for all employees to have the same "picture" of success. It allows them to understand that they are working toward a big picture and contributing to the success of that picture.

However, the most successful leaders know that sharing the vision is much stronger than just "telling" the employees about it. Truly sharing the vision allows employees to be a part of the vision. It allows employees to understand what the picture looks like, then feel invited to paint on the canvas. A leader who shares the vision and invites people to express themselves creatively about the vision will gain true commitment. The leader who has the vision and then just "tells" people what to do is just delegating tasks. The leader who shares the vision and invites people to be creative toward the vision is calling forth employees who can actually enhance the vision.

The purpose of this exercise is to allow the leader to think about how much the leader allows or invites her employees to think creatively about and contribute to her vision versus delegating tasks to get the leader's vision done. One graphic artist on my staff taught me years ago that all I needed to do was to give her a concept, and she would come up with the ideas to make the concept work. If the concept that I want to convey is hugeness, I might tell her to draw an elephant. She would probably be able to come up with 100 better ideas that would convey hugeness, but I'd never know it because I only delegated a task. When the leader conveys the concept through her vision and then allows the employees to fill in the how tos and the details, the results are much more impressive.

TRAINER'S/COACH'S NOTES

	APPROXIMATE TIME

1. Overview

Explain to the individual or group that their vision is essential. However, explain that all leaders must know how to invite their employees to share the vision. The right course of action for the leader is to outline the picture but then to invite all members of the staff to draw on the canvas to improve and color the picture.

1 minute

2. Purpose

"The purpose of this exercise is to help you determine how much of your vision you own and how much you invite others to own. Sometimes leaders enthusiastically want to own the whole vision. In doing so, they are ignoring the talents and creativity of their staff. As you invite all of your employees to share the vision and ask for their creative input into the vision, the vision gets better through synergy."

1 minute

3. Give Directions

10 minutes

A. Give the participants Exercise #32.

B. Instruct each participant to complete the worksheet by reflecting on the following:

(1) What percentage of the vision do you invent?

(2) What percentage of the vision do you invite your employees to invent?

NOTE: This exercise aims at determining leader control. Leaders who are reluctant to give up control will often be concerned about allowing employees to help invent the vision. Also, leaders who have employees whom they think are not capable performers will also be reluctant to invite employees into the vision. In those situations, the leader is more apt to delegate and structure the tasks. The coach/trainer must be sensitive to these issues in the discussion.

4. Debrief:

20 minutes

A. Have participants, in groups of four answer the following questions:

(1) What percentage of the vision do you invent? Your employees?

(2) Why are leaders sometimes reluctant to invite employees to participate in inventing the vision?

(3) What are the benefits of allowing employees to participate in inventing the vision?

B. Summarize the following points:

(1) Leaders will get more commitment from employees if they allow them to create to the vision.

(2) Leaders will get more creativity when they invite employees to create the vision versus blind delegation.

(3) Leaders are reluctant to invite employees into the vision because they are afraid to give up control of the vision.

Emotional Intelligence Exercise 32

As you think about the ways you communicate your vision, do you tell your people exactly what and how you want the vision implemented? For example, if I tell my staff:

- I want invitations printed on buff colored, recyclable paper.

- I want pictures of trees and waterfalls on the cover.

- I want to use the outdoor amphitheater at Wilson Resort for my presentation, etc.

I'm not allowing my staff much room to help create the vision. I'm just delegating. People feel more connected to the vision if they are able to be involved in filling in the details of the picture.

What percentage of your vision have you invited your employees to invent? On the pie chart below, indicate the percentage of input your employees have in filling in the details of your picture.

Example: My Percentages:

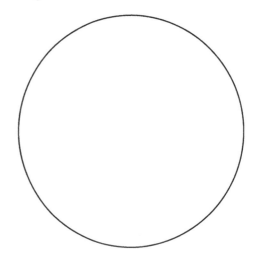

EQ #33 / Visions Apply to People Too

EQ TARGET

✓	Self-Awareness and Control
	Empathy
✓	Social Expertness
✓	Personal Influence
	Mastery of Vision

OBJECTIVES

- To help participants realize that their vision of employees has a great deal to do with the success that the employees achieve

- To help leaders recognize that when they have a negative vision of their employees, they are communicating it on some level.

ESTIMATED TIME

55 minutes

MATERIALS

Emotional Intelligence Exercise #33

RISK/DIFFICULTY

High

COACHING TIPS FOR COACH/TRAINER

Visions apply to people as well as to the work they do. When leaders have a positive vision of their people, people respond and act in a way that supports the belief. Likewise, when leaders have a negative vision of their employees or team, the team responds negatively.

The leader's perception has much to do with the performance that he receives. If leaders value and treasure their employees, they tend to treat them in a way that is consistent with this feeling. On the other hand, if leaders view their employees as a drain or a burden, then the employees' actions reflect this feeling. The emotionally competent leader knows that he must first determine the "correct" vision of his employee before being able to expect great or inspired performances. The emotionally competent leader knows that maintaining a positive, optimistic view of employees will result in building bonds with employees that will lead to greater performance.

We are not suggesting that leaders "put their heads in the sand" and ignore performance problems. If such problems exist, leaders must address them. However, there is an important distinction between addressing a performance problem and picking at performance issues. The emotionally wise leader knows to address the big issues and from there create a positive, optimistic view of performance that enables success.

The purpose of this exercise is to help leaders confront their actual view of their employees and recognize the impact of this view. An example that you could use to make the point is as follows:

Hold up a piece of artwork and tell the group that you think this is the most wonderful, inspired artwork that was ever created. If this were the case, ask the group to suggest what behaviors would follow. For example, you might display it in a prominent place; you might insure it; you might build a special shelf for it; you might show it to others; you might suggest the artist to your friends.

Hold up the same piece of artwork and tell the group that you think it is the most terrible, ugly piece of work you have ever seen. If this were the case, ask the group to suggest what behaviors might follow. For example, you might throw it in the trash; you might want your money back; you might tell your friends not to buy artwork by this artist.

The point is that our perception about something or someone will affect our behavior toward that person or thing. An important lesson for leaders is to recognize that their perception toward their employees will cause behaviors in the leader that may or may not support the cause.

TRAINER'S/COACH'S NOTES

	APPROXIMATE TIME

1. Overview

5 minutes

Explain to the individual or group that the leader's perception or vision of his employees has a great deal to do with the behaviors that he exhibits toward the employees. Explain that when the leader perceives his employees positively, the leader treats them in one way. Explain that when the leader perceives his employees negatively, the leader's behavior reflects this. Use the following example to illustrate the point:

Hold up a piece of artwork and tell the group that you think this is the most wonderful, inspired artwork that was ever created. If this were the case, ask the group to suggest what behaviors would follow. For example, you might display it in a prominent place; you might insure it; you might build a special shelf for it; you might show it to others; you might suggest the artist to your friends.

Hold up the same piece of artwork and tell the group that you think it is the most terrible, ugly piece of work you have ever seen. If this were the case, ask the group to suggest what behaviors might follow. For example, you might throw it in the trash; you might want your money back; you might tell your friends not to buy artwork by this artist.

2. Purpose

1 minute

"The purpose of this exercise is to help you recognize the vision you have of your employees and how that vision impacts them."

3. Give Directions

20 minutes

   A. Give the participants Exercise #33.

   B. Instruct each participant to complete the worksheet by answering the questions on the worksheet.

   C. Reflect on the answers.

4. Debrief:

30 minutes

   A. Have participants, in groups of four, address the following questions:

   (1) What vision would you like to have of your employees?

   (2) What is your actual vision?

   (3) How is your ideal?

   (4) Why is it important for leaders to be aware of the vision they have of their employees?

   (5) What impact can vision have on employees?

   (6) What impact can vision have on us as leaders?

B. Summarize the following points:

  (1) Your vision affects your behavior toward your employees.

  (2) Positive vision sends positive emotional signals to employees that impact performance.

  (3) Negative vision sends negative emotional signals to employees that impact performance.

Emotional Intelligence Exercise 33

What vision would you like to have of your employees? List words that describe the perfect staff.

_____

_____

_____

_____

_____

When you think about your current staff, what words actually come to mind? List these words. How does your actual vision differ from the words you listed above to describe your perfect vision?

_____

_____

_____

_____

_____

Generally, people will respond to your vision of them. Could you be communicating your actual vision versus your ideal vision? If yes, in what ways?

_____

_____

_____

_____

_____

EQ #34

Vision Spirit Killers

EQ TARGET

✓	**Self-Awareness and Control**
✓	**Empathy**
	Social Expertness
✓	**Personal Influence**
	Mastery of Vision

OBJECTIVES

- To help participants identify the known "vision spirit killers" in the workplace

- To help participants recognize that these "vision spirit killers" can create negative workplace cultures

- To help leaders recognize the "vision spirit killers" in their own behavior.

ESTIMATED TIME

45 minutes

MATERIALS

Emotional Intelligence Exercise #34

RISK/DIFFICULTY

High

COACHING TIPS FOR COACH/TRAINER

Based on our research, employees identified five "vision spirit killers" that they believe contribute to low productivity and morale. These five vision spirit killers are:

1. *Incongruent Actions*—When the boss does or says one thing and then turns around and does or reinforces the opposite, employees are quick to see the inconsistencies. High trust environments are built on consistent and congruent actions. Therefore, when actions and words are too often perceived as inconsistent, trust erodes. This erosion of trust dampers morale and creates negative emotion inconsistent with high productivity.

2. *No Action*—As common as incongruent actions are leaders who state grand visions and then take little or no action to get there. "This too shall pass" becomes the war cry of the troops who have wearily traveled this road before. It is hard to take vision statements seriously when, so often, little or nothing follows. Leaders need to act on their vision, and they need to act in a reasonable amount of time.

3. *Overcomplicating the Vision*—Sometimes leaders state visions that are so complicated we can barely read them, let alone remember them. If people can't remember the vision, chances are it isn't simple enough. Also, leaders in the middle must be careful to keep the vision simple. If you don't, no one is going to understand it and can't possibly carry it out.

4. *Lost in Detail*—Some managers are so detail-oriented that they simply can't understand the idea of vision. Minutiae consume their attention and blur the "big picture." They can't imagine there is a tomorrow they should be thinking about in a creative way. We are not suggesting that details are unimportant. They are very important. But they have to be connected to the big picture. The leader's job is to help everyone attend to the proper details, thus making the vision a reality.

5. *Sabotaging Vision*—Some, often only a few, people in the organization know the vision and understand it but work in exactly the opposite direction. They deliberately sabotage the vision. Other people in the organization know who is sabotaging the vision, and they expect that the leadership does, as well. If nothing is done to stop these efforts, then those who are putting forth genuine effort think, "What's the use?"

Adapted from *In Search of Honor: Lessons From Workers on How to Build Trust,* by Adele B. Lynn (Belle Vernon, Pa.: BajonHouse Publishing, 1998)

Emotionally intelligent leaders know that the spirit killers listed above come with a price. Therefore, the emotionally intelligent leader recognizes these vision spirit killers and works to change them.

TRAINER'S/COACH'S NOTES

	APPROXIMATE TIME
1. Overview Explain to the individual or group that the leader has to be careful of five vision spirit killers that sometimes invade workplaces. Explain the five vision spirit killers listed above to the group. Give examples of these spirit killers from your own work experience. Explain that emotionally intelligent leaders know that the spirit killers listed above come with a price. Emotionally intelligent leaders know that they must stop these from invading the workforce.	**5 minutes**
2. Purpose "The purpose of this exercise is to help you identify the vision spirit killers in your workplace and to come up with suggestions to help eliminate them."	**1 minute**

3. Give Directions
  A. Give the participants Exercise #34.
  B. Instruct participants to complete the worksheet by thinking about the vision spirit killers that may be at play in their workplace.
  C. Ask participants to come up with specific items that may be contributing to these spirit killers.
Ask participants to come up with ways to eradicate these spirit killers.
	15 minutes

4. Debrief:
  A. Have participants, in groups of four, answer the following questions:
    (1) Which vision spirit killers do you sometimes employ?
    (2) Why is it important for leaders to be aware of these five vision spirit killers?
    (3) What damage can these vision spirit killers have on employee morale?
  B. Summarize the following points:
    (1) ALL groups will experience these vision spirit killers at some time. It is when the spirit killers occur more frequently than not that permanent harm is done to the culture.
    (2) Groups are forgiving when these actions occur occasionally; however, the integrity of the leader can be harmed if they occur too frequently.
	25 minutes

Emotional Intelligence Exercise 34

Spirit Killers and Soul Suckers—The most common spirit killers regarding vision are listed below. Put a check mark next to the spirit killers that you may sometimes be guilty of employing. How can this harm employee morale? How can you eradicate these spirit killers?

- [ ] Incongruent actions

- [ ] No action

- [ ] Overcomplicating the vision

- [ ] Lost in the detail

- [ ] Allowing others to sabotage the vision

EQ #35

Advice From the Pros

EQ TARGET

✓	**Self-Awareness and Control**
	Empathy
	Social Expertness
	Personal Influence
✓	**Mastery of Vision**

OBJECTIVES

- To help participants identify actions that they could take to strengthen their vision

- To help participants gain perspective and look outside themselves to find answers to their leadership challenges.

ESTIMATED TIME

35 minutes

MATERIALS

Emotional Intelligence Exercise #35

RISK/DIFFICULTY

Low

COACHING TIPS FOR COACH/TRAINER

Most leaders already know what they should be doing to improve. This exercise allows leaders to tell themselves through the voice of a great, admired leader what they could do to improve. The leader studied in EQ 28 could be used as the advice giver.

Emotionally intelligent leaders recognize that it is OK to ask for help. They also know that, ultimately, it is within their power to make changes if they are not satisfied with the result.

The coach/trainer should act as an encourager and motivator for participants. The participants should be encouraged to implement the answers that they think will lead to the right path.

TRAINER'S/COACH'S NOTES

	APPROXIMATE TIME
1. Overview Explain to the individual or group that they can draw on resources for advice. The great leaders who were used in EQ 28 could be "called upon" at any time to give feedback to the participants if they just ask them for help.	**1 minute**
2. Purpose "The purpose of this exercise is to 'call upon' a leader that you respect or admire greatly for their visionary ability. You are going to ask that leader to help you, to critique your actions, and to otherwise give you advice on how to drive your vision to be a reality with your employees."	**1 minute**
3. Give Directions A. Give the participants Exercise #35. B. Recall the great leader that you studied in EQ 28. C. Instruct the participants to "ask" this great leader to critique and give advice to them about vision. "Ask" the great leader to tell the participant what they could do to strengthen their vision, to articulate it more clearly, to connect people with their vision, or to otherwise strengthen their position as a leader. D. Instruct each participant to write down bullet points of advice from the great leader whom they are visualizing.	**15 minutes**
4. Debrief in groups of four by asking the following questions: A. What advice did you receive from your great leader? B. Which of their suggestions would you like to implement? C. What benefit would you gain if you had a clearer vision, were able to articulate it to employees, and were able to invite employees to participate in it?	**20 minutes**

Emotional Intelligence Exercise 35

Picture Yourself—Imagine yourself having dinner with one of the great visionary leaders such as Martin Luther King, Jr., Franklin D. Roosevelt, or Fred Smith. What advice would these great visionaries give you to bolster your vision? What would they advise that would make you articulate your vision more clearly and cleverly? Which of their suggestions would you like to implement?

_____

_____

_____

_____

_____

What benefit would you gain if you had clearer vision, were able to articulate it to your employees, and were able to invite your employees into the vision?

_____

_____

_____

_____

_____

Ask yourself to commit to DOING IT!

_____

_____

_____

_____

_____

EQ #36 / Working Toward the Vision

EQ TARGET

	Self-Awareness and Control
	Empathy
	Social Expertness
✓	**Personal Influence**
✓	**Mastery of Vision**

OBJECTIVES

- To help participants determine if their employees are in line with the vision

- To help participants assess which employees are in line with the vision and which employees need to be coached toward the vision.

ESTIMATED TIME

35 minutes

MATERIALS

Emotional Intelligence Exercise #36

RISK/DIFFICULTY

Medium

COACHING TIPS FOR COACH/TRAINER

Even when the leader is doing a good job communicating the vision, not all employees are moving in the same direction or have the same understanding of it. Leaders must identify those employees who are not fully in line with the vision so that they can coach them to align with the vision.

Most of the time when employees are not in line with the vision, it is because they are not fully aware of the vision and the expectations. However, on other occasions, the leader may have to address issues related to performance, skill, or other problems that prohibit the employee from fully participating in working toward the vision.

The purpose of this exercise is to identify those employees who are not aligned with the vision in order to address strategies for recommunicating the vision. If, however, after implementing strategies to communicate the vision again, the employee still does not align with the vision, then other actions must be taken to address this problem. Those actions can include training, performance or attitude coaching, or even discipline or termination.

TRAINER'S/COACH'S NOTES

	APPROXIMATE TIME

1. Overview

Explain to the individual or group that all employees working toward a vision is a leader's dream. It is the leader's role to identify who is working and aligning themselves toward the vision and who is not. The reason the leader must determine who is not working toward the vision is so the leader can intervene and work with the team member to get him or her aligned. All members working together are a very powerful force toward achieving the vision. However, if some members are misaligned, the force toward the vision is diminished. (Show the graphic on the handout.)

2 minutes

2. Purpose

"The purpose of this exercise is to help you assess the members of your team and determine if they are aligned toward your vision. By assessing your team members' alignment, you are better prepared to coach your employees toward the vision. Sometimes your employees are hard workers who are expending much energy, but they are working toward things that are unimportant. This exercise helps you to get all team members aligned in the same direction and spend their time on the important things."

1 minute

3. Give Directions

A. Give the participants Exercise #36.

B. Instruct each participant to complete the worksheet by reflecting on each of the team members in their unit.

C. Ask the participants to draw an arrow for each team member inside the larger arrow to depict how the team member aligns with the vision.

D. For team members who are not directly aligned with the larger arrow, think about actions the leader could take to coach or counsel them to become aligned.

10 minutes

4. Debrief by asking the following questions:

A. What benefit is there in aligning all team members toward the vision?

B. What strategies could you use to align team members?

C. What obstacles prevent people from aligning with the vision?

D. How could you remove those obstacles?

25 minutes

Emotional Intelligence Exercise 36

If the large arrow demonstrates the direction of your vision, draw smaller arrows inside the vision to depict the direction in which your employees are working toward the vision. Label each smaller arrow with the names of your employees.

Example:

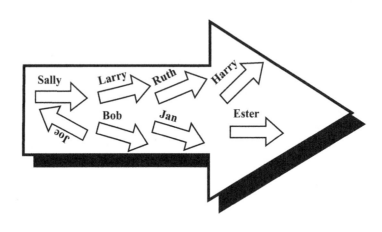

My Staff:

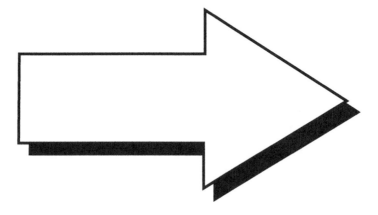

EQ #37 Advice From Employees

EQ #37

EQ TARGET

✓	Self-Awareness and Control
	Empathy
	Social Expertness
✓	Personal Influence
✓	Mastery of Vision

OBJECTIVES

- To help participants gain personal awareness of some of the vision killers that employees perceive in the workplace

- To help participants assess their personal strengths and weaknesses related to vision

- To help participants determine actions that they would like to change related to vision.

ESTIMATED TIME

40 minutes

MATERIALS

Emotional Intelligence Exercise #37

RISK/DIFFICULTY

High

COACHING TIPS FOR COACH/TRAINER

Employees have named ten behaviors that they believe kill a sense of vision in a work group. These actions are behaviors that the leader can influence. Emotionally intelligent leaders know that their behavior influences perceptions. These perceptions are critical to motivating employees toward the vision. However, most leaders don't think about vision in terms of behavior, so they may be unaware that certain behaviors can affect people's commitment toward the vision.

The top ten vision killers identified by employees include the following actions by leaders:

1. Treating people badly, such as not showing them they care, forgetting to say thank you, not respecting people, not making people feel valued.

2. Not setting good examples and living by the adage, "Do as I say, not as I do."

3. Focusing on too many things at once.

4. Pushing too hard on the task and forgetting the people.

5. Not giving clear direction.

6. Giving inconsistent direction.

7. Not taking responsibility for failure.

8. Focusing on the detail and forgetting to tell the "whys" or the big picture.

9. Showing little or no personal commitment to the vision.

10. Allowing people who aren't performing the job to remain.

In the eyes of employees, these 10 items ranked highest in reasons why people felt less committed and less connected to the leader's vision.

Adapted from *In Search of Honor: Lessons From Workers on How to Build Trust,* by Adele B. Lynn (Belle Vernon, PA.: BajonHouse Publishing, 1998).

TRAINER'S/COACH'S NOTES

	APPROXIMATE TIME
1. Overview	**5 minutes**
Explain to the individual or groups that the leader's behavior has much to do with how committed employees are toward the vision. Explain that the emotionally intelligent leader knows that certain behaviors impact employee commitment. List the top ten reasons that people feel less committed to a vision. Explain that often leaders believe that the employee needs to get with it, but that the leader's behavior may be signaling something else.	
2. Purpose	**1 minute**
"The purpose of this exercise is to help you assess your own behavior to determine if something in your behavior may be sending mixed signals about your vision to your employees. Employees who were surveyed listed the top ten reasons why they felt less committed or aligned to a vision. These reasons reflect behaviors that are within the leader's power to change. In this exercise, level with yourself to determine if something you may be doing may be working counter to your goals."	
3. Give Directions	**10 minutes**
A. Give the participants Exercise #37.	
B. Instruct each participant to complete the worksheet by reflecting on each of the items and placing a check mark on the continuum to indicate how often or seldom the leader engages in this behavior.	
C. Ask the participants to reflect on their three worst scores.	
4. Debrief by asking the following questions:	**25 minutes**
A. What are your three worst scores?	
B. What impact can the leader's behavior have on the employee's willingness to commit?	
C. What impact do the items listed have on your behavior when you are a follower?	
D. Would some of your employees be impacted negatively by your behavior?	
E. What can you do to change the situation?	

Emotional Intelligence Exercise 37

Based on our research, we've listed the top ten vision killers. For each vision killer, place a mark on the continuum below to indicate how often or seldom you engage in this activity. Leaders kill a vision by:

1. Treating people badly, such as not showing them they care, forgetting to say thank you, not respecting people, not making people feel valued.

   very seldom   very often

2. Not setting good examples and living by the adage "Do as I say, not as I do."

   very seldom   very often

3. Focusing on too many things at once.

   very seldom   very often

4. Pushing too hard on the task and forgetting the people.

   very seldom   very often

5. Not giving clear directions.

   very seldom   very often

6. Giving inconsistent direction.

   very seldom   very often

7. Not taking responsibility for failure.

   very seldom   very often

8. Focusing on the detail and forgetting to tell the "whys" or the big picture.

   very seldom   very often

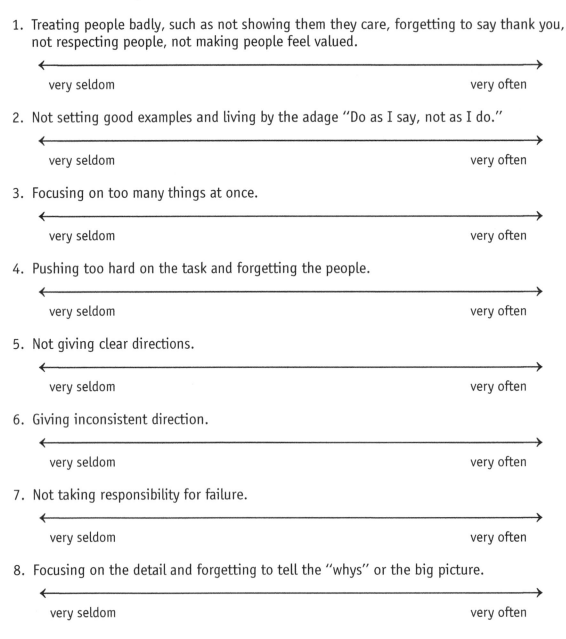

9. Showing little or no personal commitment to the vision.

$\longleftarrow$ ———————————————————————— $\longrightarrow$

very seldom   very often

10. Allowing people who aren't performing the job to remain.

$\longleftarrow$ ———————————————————————— $\longrightarrow$

very seldom   very often

EQ #38

Today's Actions Toward the Vision

EQ TARGET

	Self-Awareness and Control
	Empathy
	Social Expertness
✓	**Personal Influence**
✓	**Mastery of Vision**

OBJECTIVES

- To help participants determine if they are taking daily actions toward the vision

- To help participants assess which actions seem to be working to engage people toward the vision.

ESTIMATED TIME

35 minutes

MATERIALS

Emotional Intelligence Exercise #38

RISK/DIFFICULTY

Medium

COACHING TIPS FOR COACH/TRAINER

It's easy for leaders to think that once they state the vision, their job is finished. They may believe it is up to the employees to carry on in the direction of the vision. Not so. Every day, every leader must re-communicate, realign, or otherwise remind people about the direction. A constant, encouraging, clamoring by the leader restating the vision in a variety of different phrases helps people to connect to the vision.

Restating the vision is especially necessary when people are not 100 percent aligned or when the leader is expanding or changing the vision. Of course, the best results will occur when the leader is demonstrating all other components of emotional intelligence, such as building bonds and encouraging high trust. Fundamentally, the leader's job is to inspire people toward a goal. Unless that goal is firmly communicated and planted in the team, the leader will not achieve success.

TRAINER'S/COACH'S NOTES

	APPROXIMATE TIME

1. Overview

1 minute

Explain to the individual or group that many leaders think that visioning is something that can be crossed off the things-to-do list. Instead, visioning is something that the leader has to do in small and different ways everyday. Most leaders get lost in what they consider to be "work" and forget that instilling the vision is probably one of the most important aspects of their work.

2. Purpose

1 minute

"The purpose of this exercise is to help you assess the amount of work you do toward your vision each day. If all members of your team are perfectly aligned with the vision, you probably have little work to do here. However, most of us have team members who need to be reminded, encouraged, and prodded toward the vision. Also, change is a constant factor in most of our environments and brings a need to reiterate the vision. Reinforcing the vision also strengthens everyone's belief that the leader is committed to the vision."

3. Give Directions

5 minutes*

A. Give the participants Exercise #38.

B. Instruct each participant to complete the worksheet over a two-week period.

***Denotes classroom time**

C. Ask the participants to list things they have done over the last two-week period that support their vision. It could be talking with employees in a meeting, talking one-to-one with employees, reinforcing actions, or otherwise supporting the vision. Ask participants to be specific and to tell specific actions that they have taken with employees to advance their vision.

D. Analyze the logs at the end of the two-week period to determine if there are time gaps when leaders ignored the vision. Also, ask participants to put a star next to the items that they think had the largest impact on reinforcing or communicating their vision.

4. Debrief by asking the following questions:

30 minutes

A. What gaps were evident?

B. What actions proved strongest to moving the vision forward?

C. How do you know that these actions impacted the vision?

D. Where do you need to pay more attention to the vision?

Emotional Intelligence Exercise 38

Keep the following log for a two-week period. Note at least one visible action you have taken each day that communicates your passion for the vision.

DAY	ACTION
Sunday	
Monday	
Tuesday	
Wednesday	
Thursday	
Friday	
Saturday	
Sunday	
Monday	
Tuesday	
Wednesday	
Thursday	
Friday	
Saturday	

Analyze your log and determine if you have any gaps. Put a star next to those items that had the most impact.

EQ #39

Fuel the Vision

EQ TARGET

✓	Self-Awareness and Control
	Empathy
	Social Expertness
✓	Personal Influence
	Mastery of Vision

OBJECTIVES

- To help participants learn some methods recommended by employees that can be used to fuel the vision

- To help participants assess areas they could implement for increasing vision.

ESTIMATED TIME

45 minutes

MATERIALS

Emotional Intelligence Exercise #39

RISK/DIFFICULTY

Medium

COACHING TIPS FOR COACH/TRAINER

More than 1,000 employees interviewed netted the following advice for leaders. The employees were giving advice on how to encourage the best performance from workers. That advice included the following:

1. Leaders should believe in themselves and in their message.

2. Ask employees how to make it work.

3. Lovingly shout, "No, no! Wrong direction!" Don't expect employees to know if you haven't told them.

4. Set the example.

5. Act as if you care.

6. Direct and focus the energy in the same direction simultaneously.

7. Deal with the people who aren't doing the job.

8. Don't give employees inconsistent messages.

9. Ask employees what is going wrong. Stick around and listen to the answers.

10. Take responsibility for failure.

11. Give employees the big picture.

12. Believe in your employees.

Adapted from *In Search of Honor: Lessons From Workers on How to Build Trust,* by Adele B. Lynn (Belle Vernon, Pa.: BajonHouse Publishers, 1998).

If the leader were tuned into the advice of their own employees, they might very well encounter some of the same statements. This survey can help leaders understand some of the concerns that may exist within their own work unit.

The purpose of this exercise is to help leaders become more sensitive and aware of employee issues and concerns.

TRAINER'S/COACH'S NOTES

	APPROXIMATE TIME

1. Overview

5 minutes

Explain to the individual or group that employees' opinions about what motivates them is important information for the leader to consider. Explain that sometimes it is useful for leaders to consider this data so they are better able to empathize and build bonds that will result in motivated employees. Share the survey results from the Trainer's/Coach's Notes with the group.

2. Purpose

1 minute

"The purpose of this exercise is to help you to consider information about motivation that may strengthen you as a leader. The information resulted from the opinions of more than 1,000 workers from a variety of industries. The employees surveyed were asked to describe the conditions that bring out the best performance in people from the employee's point of view. In this exercise, you will consider the opinions of these workers and decide if there are some items that you would like to improve in your leadership behavior."

3. Give Directions

20 minutes

A. Give the participants Exercise #39.

B. Instruct each participant to complete the worksheet by reflecting on the advice listed on the page.

C. Ask participants to put a check mark next to any of the items they would like to implement (or strengthen existing behaviors).

D. Ask the participants to write an action plan with some ideas on how they could implement the advice in their work areas.

4. Debrief by asking the following questions:

20 minutes

A. From the list of advice, what items would you like to implement or strengthen?

B. How do you intend to implement the items you marked?

C. Would your employees have similar statements of advice if asked? Please explain.

Emotional Intelligence Exercise 39

Consider the following list of advice from employees on how to fuel the vision. Put a check mark next to the top three items that you would like to implement more often.

_____   1. Believe in yourself and your message.

_____   2. Ask us how to make it work.

_____   3. Lovingly shout, "No, no! Wrong direction!" Don't expect us to know if you haven't told us.

_____   4. Set the example.

_____   5. Act as if you care.

_____   6. Direct and focus our energy in the same direction simultaneously.

_____   7. Deal with people who aren't doing the job.

_____   8. Don't give us inconsistent messages.

_____   9. Ask us what is going wrong.

_____ 10. Take responsibility for failure.

_____ 11. Give us the big picture.

_____ 12. Believe in us.

How do you intend to implement the items you checked? Write an action plan for implementing the advice. Be specific.

_____

_____

_____

_____

_____

_____

EQ #40

Picture Yourself

EQ TARGET

	Self-Awareness and Control
	Empathy
	Social Expertness
✓	**Personal Influence**
✓	**Mastery of Vision**

OBJECTIVES

- To help participants prioritize their energy

- To help participants determine what actions could best further their vision.

ESTIMATED TIME

50 minutes

MATERIALS

Emotional Intelligence Exercise #40

RISK/DIFFICULTY

Medium

COACHING TIPS FOR COACH/TRAINER

If only there were enough hours in the day, then the leader would have time to do everything necessary to further the vision. Of course, all leaders face difficult priorities and tasks competing for their attention. However, fueling the vision is essential to leadership. Leaders must have and demonstrate passion toward the vision every day in order for employees to commit.

This exercise is aimed at helping leaders visualize themselves doing positive actions. Visualizing oneself in successful situations helps people to commit to goals and also helps motivate people. Leaders who visualize themselves taking positive steps to achieve their goals are more apt to act on the visualizations.

TRAINER'S/COACH'S NOTES

	APPROXIMATE TIME

1. Overview
1 minute

Explain to the individual or group that visualizing is a powerful tool for development. Tell the group that many great athletes use visualization to improve their skills.

2. Purpose
2 minutes

"The purpose of this exercise is to help you to picture yourself doing things that further your goals in the workplace. By using visualization, you will picture yourself taking positive actions that will serve to promote your vision with your employees. For example, if you think that you need to stop to talk to people more frequently as you walk through the work area, visualizing this activity will help you remember to do so. Visualizing it will also help you to know what to say, how to say it, and to whom you want to speak. Visualization serves as the mind's cue to take the action that was mentally rehearsed. These mental rehearsals serve to build your skill and motivation."

3. Give Directions
20–30 minutes

A. Give the participants Exercise #40.

B. Instruct participants to visualize themselves having unlimited energy to do what is required to move their goals forward.

C. Ask them to see themselves as a leader with unlimited energy and stamina.

D. Ask participants to state what they see themselves doing each day that they currently don't have time to do.

E. Ask participants to very clearly picture themselves doing things that are moving their work unit toward their goals.

F. Ask participants to write down what they pictured themselves doing during the visualization.

NOTE: Allow adequate time for the visualization to continue. (At least 15 minutes is suggested.) Continue to ask the participants to state what they see themselves doing. Keep pressing by asking "what else?"

4. Debrief by asking the following questions:
15 minutes

A. What could you do to energize your vision?

B. What obstacles are holding you back from the actions you saw in your visualization?

C. What benefits would occur if you acted on the visualizations?

D. Who could help you overcome the obstacles?

Emotional Intelligence Exercise 40

Picture Yourself—Imagine yourself as having unlimited energy. What could you do to energize your vision that you just can't seem to find time to do today? Write it down. What's stopping you from doing it right now? Work to find a solution to your roadblocks. Talk with a mentor, your boss, or other significant person who can help you overcome these roadblocks. Ask yourself to commit to DOING IT!

EQ #41

Lessons From Low Points/High Points

EQ TARGET

✓	Self-Awareness and Control
	Empathy
	Social Expertness
✓	Personal Influence
	Mastery of Vision

OBJECTIVES

- To deepen participants' awareness of the significance of being a leader

- To help participants learn from previous experiences, both good and bad, and draw on those experiences to become better leaders.

ESTIMATED TIME

60 minutes

MATERIALS

Emotional Intelligence Exercise #41

RISK/DIFFICULTY

High

COACHING TIPS FOR COACH/TRAINER

Personal experiences can be a rich training ground if used to reflect on things done well and things that could be improved. Being a leader is a difficult task, and learning to master leadership from books alone is just not practical. Books can enhance learning, but experiences and reactions to them can build important lessons in leadership.

Reflecting on high points and low points as a leader will help improve self awareness. When leaders internalize these lessons and change their leadership based on past mistakes and successes, leaders stand to become even more effective.

This exercise is based on self-reflection about leaders' past achievements and failures. The purpose of reflection is to learn from errors and to build on successes.

When facilitating or coaching people on self-reflection, it is important to create a learning environment that is not judgmental or critical. You should try to create an atmosphere in which participants can openly discuss their failures and successes. Sometimes, depending on the dynamics within an organization, this is difficult to do in an in-house session. You will have to use your judgment to determine if this will work in a group setting. If not, this exercise can definitely be conducted in house on a private coaching basis.

TRAINER'S/COACH'S NOTES

	APPROXIMATE TIME

1. Overview

Explain to the individual or group that experience is often the best teacher. However, experience is also worthless unless you learn from the past. Forced reflection on your successes and failures can help you achieve a blueprint for success in your future if you diligently consider what your successes and failures have to teach you. Therefore, if you treat your past as a rich source of information to help you become more effective, then visiting your successes and failures can be a rewarding experience. However, it is important to visit your past in the right frame of mind. Your frame of mind should not be judgmental or critical, simply open to learning. Explain that sometimes when you experience failures, you want to bury them and forget them. In doing so, you miss an important opportunity to learn from your failures.

2 minutes

2. Purpose

"The purpose of this exercise is to help you consider the lessons in your past experiences. These lessons can be very effective in helping you become better leaders. Whether you have had good experiences or negative ones, lessons await. If you can look at these lessons and use the information to modify your leadership actions, you have much to gain. However, without reflecting on your past experiences, you have no mechanism for learning from your mistakes or your successes. Therefore, this exercise is aimed at helping you reflect on your experiences so that you can create lessons that are worth incorporating into your future. Sometimes, it might be painful to look at your failures, but by forcing yourself to do just this, you stand to gain a great deal."

1 minute

3. Give Directions

A. Give the participants Exercise #41.

B. Instruct each participant to complete the worksheet by reflecting on the questions. Allow individuals time to reflect in private on these questions.

C. Ask the participants to draw an "x" on the continuum to indicate their level of satisfaction with the leader they have become.

D. Also, ask participants to reflect on the leaders they would like to become. What lessons must they internalize in order for their goals to be reached?

20 minutes

4. Debrief by asking the following questions:

A. What lessons from your low points should you try to incorporate in your future?

B. What lessons from your high points should you try to incorporate in your future?

40 minutes

C. Were their patterns in your low points? Did you repeat certain actions or attitudes that were destructive?

D. Were their patterns in your high points? Did you repeat certain actions or attitudes that were constructive?

E. How satisfied are you with the leader you have become? Please explain.

F. What would improve your satisfaction level with yourself?

Emotional Intelligence Exercise 41

Consider a few of your low points related to being boss. Reflect deeply on these times. What can you learn about yourself from these low points? Write down at least two lessons.

_____

_____

_____

_____

Consider some of your high points related to being a boss. Reflect deeply on these times. What can you learn about yourself from these high points? Write down at least two lessons.

_____

_____

_____

_____

On the continuum below, place an x on the line that indicates your level of personal satisfaction with the leader you have become.

← _____ →

very dissatisfied   very satisfied

In the previous question, what would make your x move up the scale?

_____

_____

_____

_____

EQ #42

It's My Show

EQ TARGET

✓	Self-Awareness and Control
	Empathy
	Social Expertness
	Personal Influence
✓	Mastery of Vision

OBJECTIVES

- To deepen participants' awareness of the need for leaders' actions and beliefs to be congruent
- To help participants learn that ultimately leaders must find their own style
- To encourage leaders to think about the importance of independent thinking.

ESTIMATED TIME

60 minutes

MATERIALS

Emotional Intelligence Exercise #42

RISK/DIFFICULTY

High

COACHING TIPS FOR COACH/TRAINER

It is important for each leader to build a strong personal philosophy grounded in the leader's sense of values and judgment. Although relying on mentors and others for guidance is certainly a worthwhile way to gain insights and learn, ultimately, each leader must grow into her own set of belief systems that guide the leader's actions. Sometimes the development of these belief systems is thwarted because leaders "grow up" in certain organizations and those belief systems are adopted as their own without the benefit of determining if they actually fit their personal belief systems. If the organizational belief systems do not fit their own belief systems, then leaders often appear incongruent to their followers.

Incongruent actions can cause followers to get the sense that leaders are "not real." That something that they project is not in line with what they believe. Followers are quick to notice these inconsistencies and will often label these leaders as "cardboard cutouts," because they do not know what they truly believe and act only on what the company tells them to believe. That's not to say that all leaders must not at times take actions that are not totally consistent with their belief system. Of course, part of being a good follower demands this at times. However, when this occurs, the strong self-assured leader understands the compromise and is willing to make it because she also can see some benefit.

This exercise is aimed at helping leaders determine what their personal belief system is and how that personal belief system either meshes with the organization's belief system or opposes it. All emotionally intelligent leaders know what their personal belief system is and how it guides their actions as a leader. Those leaders who are most effective are in organizations (or have created organizations) where the belief system is consistent with their own.

It is possible that this exercise could bring to the attention of the leader some serious considerations about the fit between herself and the organization in which she works.

TRAINER'S/COACH'S NOTES

	APPROXIMATE TIME
1. Overview	**2 minutes**

Explain to the individual or group that emotionally intelligent leaders have a strong understanding of what they believe in. They are able to articulate their beliefs, they recognize when their beliefs are being compromised, and they are able to give reasons why they believe what they do. These leaders have well-developed philosophies about how to treat people and how to run an organization to get the best results. These leaders draw on their belief systems when in doubt about a particular situation. Even if they make mistakes, their followers perceive them as being sincere. They are not perceived as yes people or sheep, but instead can look at a situation with their own set of beliefs and act accordingly. This strong sense of self gives followers the impression of inner strength. This type of leader does not need to rely on external power or authority because she knows that her true power comes from this belief system.

2. Purpose	**2 minutes**

"The purpose of this exercise is to help you to determine what your individual beliefs are in relation to leadership. You will be asked to think about your individual beliefs and how they are similar or different from your organization's beliefs, or your boss's beliefs, or even that of a mentor or friend. By admitting how your beliefs differ from others, your position and beliefs become solidified. A solid belief system shows itself as self-confidence and inner power in the leader. Followers can quickly determine which leaders believe what they are doing/saying and distinguish them from those who just follow the organizational line. Also, leaders whose belief system is congruent with the organization or company in which they lead are satisfied that they are not selling out and thus are more effective leaders."

3. Give Directions	**20 minutes**

    A. Give the participants Exercise #42.

    B. Instruct each participant to complete the worksheet by reflecting on the questions. Allow individuals time to reflect in private on these questions.

    C. Encourage participants to think deeply about the questions and to extend their thinking to many different facets of the organization.

    D. Encourage participants to think about how they would run the show.

4. Debrief by asking the following questions:	**40 minutes**

    A. What are some examples you have listed that don't fit within your belief system?

    B. How do these items differ from your personal belief system?

    C. When did imitating someone's style prove successful? Unsuccessful?

D. How can imitating another person's leadership style help you to determine your own?

E. What different actions would you take if you "ran the show?"

F. Are the compromises that you make within your organization causing you to live outside your own belief system? Is this occurring so frequently that you feel as though you are compromising who you are? Please elaborate.

Emotional Intelligence Exercise 42

Whether you've been a leader for a lifetime or for just a few short weeks, reflect on your role as a leader and consider some ideas you tried to implement that just didn't/don't make sense to you. Perhaps it's a company policy that seems stupid, or a boss's suggestion on how to address a people problem, or a book you've read that seems off base. These are ideas, suggestions, or actions that are incongruent with your beliefs. List some examples here. Analyze these examples to determine why they don't seem right to you.

_____

_____

_____

_____

Think about times when you have tried to imitate someone else's leadership style. When was it successful? When was it unsuccessful?

_____

_____

_____

_____

If you had no one to answer to, what would you do differently. In other words, if you were your own boss and ran the show completely and independently, how would you lead differently? In what areas do you feel your hands are tied? How would you make changes? (Some of you may already have this luxury; for others, this exercise could be very useful.)

_____

_____

_____

_____

EQ #43

Interior Power

EQ TARGET

✓	**Self-Awareness and Control**
	Empathy
	Social Expertness
✓	**Personal Influence**
✓	**Mastery of Vision**

OBJECTIVES

- To introduce the concept of interior power and its impact on leadership
- To help participants determine ways to strengthen their interior power.

ESTIMATED TIME

60 minutes

MATERIALS

Emotional Intelligence Exercise #43

RISK/DIFFICULTY

High

COACHING TIPS FOR COACH/TRAINER

Ours is a society obsessed with the words and the deeds of power. We have it, lose it, need it, want it, and abuse it. However, power is not a thing to have, to abuse, to need, or to want. It is, instead, something that flows from a well-cultivated self, a self that is assured and confident in its actions. Ultimately, it is the only true power anyone has.

When a leader has this interior power, it is obvious to those around him. People are drawn to it. This inner strength calls others like a magnet. Those around it feel the strength, the presence, the confidence. Within this interior power are the true roots of leadership. Interior power is the source from which the leader will draw all other dimensions of leadership. It is from here that vision, direction, and inspiration are seeded.

Followers want leaders who know the way. If they don't know the way, then followers at least want leaders who can find the way. "Confident" doesn't mean that the leader has all the answers. It simply means that he is committed and believes he can find the answers. It also doesn't imply control. In fact, the most confident leaders are the most empowering.

This exercise is aimed at beginning the discussion of interior power with the leader. Every leader must think deeply about the concept of interior power and must find the source and strength of that interior power.

You should begin the discussion of interior power by allowing the leader to define what he thinks the concept means and then by asking how much interior power the leader perceives himself to possess. The fruits of the discussion are in the leader defining power for himself.

TRAINER'S/COACH'S NOTES

	APPROXIMATE TIME

1. Overview — 2 minutes

Explain to the individual or group that true power can come only from within. That, ultimately, the leader cannot rely on external means or position as a source of power to be most effective. Also, explain that emotionally intelligent leaders have a very well-developed sense of interior power and are able to draw on it for their most daunting leadership tasks. Interior power doesn't fail because it is based on a strong sense of self. Discuss the notion that some leaders who lack interior power are often those who feel a strong sense of control or those who often speak or shout the loudest. Also, discuss the notion that the most empowering leaders have a well-developed sense of interior power.

2. Purpose — 2 minutes

"The purpose of this exercise is to help you consider your own source of interior power. How does this interior power translate into your leadership style? Also, this exercise is just the beginning of a long quest to further develop your interior power. Emotionally intelligent leaders think about how they can be more effective every day and in so doing must question the concept of power. Those who are most successful know that power is not something to have, to gain, or to use. It is only something that comes from within and displays itself to others through a strong sense of beliefs and inner confidence."

3. Give Directions — 20 minutes

A. Give the participants Exercise #43.

B. Instruct each participant to complete the worksheet by reflecting on the questions. Allow individuals time to reflect in private on these questions.

4. Debrief by asking the following questions: — 15 minutes

A. How strong is your interior power?

B. How would you define interior power?

C. What do you think interior power has to do with leadership?

D. What methods can you use to improve your interior power?

E. How do followers know when a leader has a strong sense of interior power?

F. How do followers know when a leader has a weak sense of interior power?

Emotional Intelligence Exercise 43

How strong is your sense of interior power? Place a mark on the gauge below to indicate your level of interior power.

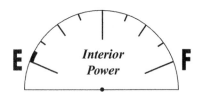

How would you define interior power?

_____

_____

_____

_____

What do you think interior power has to do with leadership?

_____

_____

_____

_____

How do you think you can increase interior power?

_____

_____

_____

_____

EQ #44 / Control and Empowerment

EQ TARGET

✓	**Self-Awareness and Control**
✓	**Empathy**
	Social Expertness
✓	**Personal Influence**
	Mastery of Vision

OBJECTIVES

■ To encourage participants to be aware of their need for control

■ To determine the primary reasons we wish to control others and to examine the impact of that control.

ESTIMATED TIME

55 minutes

MATERIALS

Emotional Intelligence Exercise #44

RISK/DIFFICULTY

High

COACHING TIPS FOR COACH/TRAINER

Exploring the relationship between leadership and control is central to every leader's growth. Every leader must eventually confront his or her understanding of this relationship. Leaders err on both sides. There are those who attempt to overcontrol and seek to manipulate their followers' every action. On the other hand, a leader who is "in control" demonstrates a strong sense of interior power that helps others become empowered.

Excessive control of others suggests a lack of interior power. People who need to control everything in their environment—the people, the events, the places—are most often insecure. They have a basic disbelief and distrust of self and others that translates into very disempowering feelings.

True interior power sparks power in others. It can be given away freely and will come back with great return. It is the essence of empowerment. Empowering means enabling others to do their jobs to the best of their ability. What better way to enable than to help spark the power of others—to give to others the permission to use their interior strength to accomplish the task at hand.

This exercise examines the leader's relationship to control. You may wish to tie this to other assessments or leadership style exercises that examine control issues.

TRAINER'S/COACH'S NOTES

	APPROXIMATE TIME

1. Overview

1 minute

Explain to the individual or group that many leaders have a very strong need to control others. Unfortunately, that control can often kill creativity, self motivation, and innovation in followers because it does not permit them to contribute and think. However, if leaders examine their relationship to control, they can also overcome these characteristics that may be less than ideal for followers. Also, leaders who bring forth the best in their people are able to "give away" their power and control but still maintain a strong sense of leadership and direction.

2. Purpose

1 minute

"The purpose of this exercise is to help you consider how strong your need for control is with the people whom you lead. Also, this exercise will help you to consider the impact of your need to control. In addition, it is important for you to recognize that your need for control may be different for different people. Usually this difference is attributed to the fact that you have a different comfort level with the person's ability or skills. When this occurs, you may be able to look at methods that could help empower the individual by building the person's skill."

3. Give Directions

15 minutes

A. Give the participants Exercise #44.

B. Instruct each participant to complete the worksheet by reflecting on the questions. Allow individuals time to reflect in private on these questions.

C. Be sure to encourage participants to indicate by name the persons they control the most/least.

D. Also, encourage participants to reflect on the reasons "why" they disempower some employees. The reason could indicate that some other action is needed with those particular followers.

4. Debrief by asking the following questions:

40 minutes

A. What differences did you notice in your need to control employees?

B. Was your need to control proportional to your confidence in the person's ability to do the job? Please elaborate.

C. Was your need to control proportional to your trust level regarding this person's attitude? For example, those people with a negative attitude often provoke feelings of control in the leader because the leader is concerned that this negative attitude may show up with customers or with other people in the organization. Please explain.

D. Rather than just "letting go," what actions could you take with the employee whom you have indicated a strong need to control? For example, would skill training help ease your need to control? Would creating a more trustworthy relationship ease your need to control?

E. What other strategies could you use with employees whom you have a strong need to control?

Emotional Intelligence Exercise 44

On the continuum below, place an x on the line to indicate your need to control people or situations.

← ——— →

strong need
to control

little need
to control

Would your staff see you as empowering? Write each staff person's name on the left, then to the right, mark the continuum with an x to indicate how empowered that staff person would consider you to be.

Name _____

← ——————————————————— →

strong need
to control

little need
to control

Name _____

← ——————————————————— →

strong need
to control

little need
to control

Name _____

← ——————————————————— →

strong need
to control

little need
to control

Name _____

← ——————————————————— →

strong need
to control

little need
to control

Name _____

← ——————————————————— →

strong need
to control

little need
to control

Name _____

← ——————————————————— →

strong need
to control

little need
to control

Whom do you disempower? Write their names below. Why do you disempower them?

EQ #45

Steps for Growth

EQ TARGET

✓	Self-Awareness and Control
	Empathy
	Social Expertness
	Personal Influence
✓	Mastery of Vision

OBJECTIVES

- To help participants establish a pattern for assessing their personal learning as it relates to leadership

- To help participants realize that the principles of lifelong learning apply to leadership.

ESTIMATED TIME

50 minutes

MATERIALS

Emotional Intelligence Exercise #45

RISK/DIFFICULTY

High

COACHING TIPS FOR COACH/TRAINER

The path to becoming a better leader can take many different avenues. However, the important thing isn't what path to take, but to get started and to keep moving. Emotionally intelligent leaders are always reevaluating to determine lessons learned. Emotionally intelligent leaders also have a method for assessing their learning. They do not mull other failures and become frozen; instead, they use the learning to become better. Likewise, they don't rest on their success but instead build most successes into future ones.

As the coach or trainer, your role should be one of encouraging inquiry and growth, of supporting learning. The important principle to instill is to always encourage the leader to improve.

The exercise suggests a five-step method for growth based on the author's findings. As you work with your leaders, these five steps could become central to their learning. However, whatever method you pursue, encourage the leaders to continually assess their development and look for ways to improve.

TRAINER'S/COACH'S NOTES

	APPROXIMATE TIME
1. Overview Explain to the individual or group that learning is a continuous and lifelong process. Encourage the leaders to experience learning for the sake of pure fun. The added benefit to this continuous learning is that eventually, the job of leader gets a little easier. It becomes a little less confusing as belief systems develop and leadership becomes more natural. However, stress that all leaders, especially the best leaders, see their growth as a continuous work in progress. Explain that leaders are never finished with the task of becoming better, but rather are just somewhere along the path.	**1 minute**
2. Purpose "The purpose of this exercise is to give each of you a method or process for considering your experiences and learning from them. Any method may work; this method is just easy to follow, and we encourage you to try it. The steps of the method are: ■ Seek comments ■ Reflect ■ Study past lessons ■ Picture yourself and laugh ■ Give yourself permission to grow." (Explain each step based on the worksheet handout.)	**5 minutes**

3. Give Directions
    A. Give the participants Exercise #45.
    B. Instruct each participant to complete the worksheet by reflecting on the questions in the five-step process. Allow individuals time to reflect in private on these questions.
    C. Encourage participants to use this method each week for a month. (Some participants use this method every day.)
 	
NOTE: Occasionally leaders have trouble understanding the rationale for using humor (Step 4—Picture yourself and laugh.) Humor helps in two specific ways: (1) Tying our actions to something funny helps us remember our areas of growth. For example, one problem that I often have is my impetuous nature to have things immediately even though there really is no rush. When I picture myself as the White Rabbit in *Alice in Wonderland,* I make myself look absurd and am able to remember to ease up. (2) We need to forgive ourselves for our mistakes. Humor lightens up our errors and says, move on, and get past it.
	10 minutes

4. Debrief by asking the following questions: A. What methods do you use to seek comment?	**35 minutes**

B. What methods of reflection do you use?

C. What can you learn from past mistakes?

D. How can you find ways to look at your humorous side?

E. How have you given yourself permission to grow?

F. What benefit can you see to some routine way of assessing our life's lessons?

Emotional Intelligence Exercise 45

1. *Seek Comment*—My favorite steps are to ask people who think highly of me for feedback. Then, I make it a point to ask those people who I think have a low opinion of me. (That's a tough one, and I still struggle through it, but I have discovered some very important information from these people.) Who/what can you ask/do to gain comments?

_____

_____

_____

_____

2. *Reflect*—For years, my favorite way to reflect has been by keeping a journal. I find that the act of hashing out on paper my deepest concerns and thoughts is invaluable. I also like to walk in the woods with my dog. What methods of reflection do you find valuable? Whatever the method, I suggest you do it daily.

_____

_____

_____

_____

3. *Study Past Lessons*—Making mistakes is part of living. I'm not advocating perfection. However, when we keep making the same mistakes as a leader, we need some method of learning from these past mistakes. I keep a log of lessons learned in my journal. Then, especially before a task or assignment where I anticipate difficulty, I review my journal to find the wisdom I need to get through. What can you do to learn from your past mistakes?

_____

_____

_____

_____

4. *Picture Yourself and Laugh*—It's important to take ourselves seriously as a leader, but I also find great benefit in finding the humor in who I am as a leader. My favorite technique is to picture my absurd actions in the form of cartoon characters. I cut these characters out and hang them in a visible location as a reminder to lighten up. How can you find ways to look at your humorous side as a leader?

_____

_____

_____

_____

5. *Give Yourself Permission to Grow*—When you think for yourself, you sometimes upset the norms of the past and the people who have set them. Being a leader is about confronting those norms, accepting those that make sense, then permitting yourself to create new norms that are right for you. Are you holding on to things that you need to release? Do you need to create new ideas or ways that are distinctively yours? Give yourself permission to do just that.

_____

_____

_____

_____

Adapted from *In Search of Honor: Lessons From Workers on How to Build Trust,* by Adele B. Lynn (Belle Vernon, Pa.: BajonHouse, 1998).

EQ #46 / Spirit Killers That Stunt Your Growth

EQ TARGET

✓	**Self-Awareness and Control**
	Empathy
	Social Expertness
	Personal Influence
✓	**Mastery of Vision**

OBJECTIVES

- To help participants discuss and consider the most common spirit killers that stunt a leader's growth

- To help participants strategize ways to stop the spirit killers from robbing their development as leaders.

ESTIMATED TIME

50 minutes

MATERIALS

Emotional Intelligence Exercise #46

RISK/DIFFICULTY

High

COACHING TIPS FOR COACH/TRAINER

As the quest to become great leaders continues, it is worthwhile to note that certain "spirit killers" can ruin leaders' chances of success. Awareness of these spirit killers can help thwart their pernicious hold. The most common spirit killers that thwart growth are:

Celebrity Ego—Everyone knows someone whose "EGO" is too big. Egotism is a major spirit killer. It's our egotism that holds us back from learning more about ourselves. If we already believe that we are great, then why would we consider changing? This blocks us from listening to the truth, and the bigger the "EGO," the larger the block. If we would just drop the celebrity status and work to be real, then we just might grow. Interestingly, leaders sometimes adopt this celebrity status because they really don't know any other way to be. They are playing the "role."

Fear—The greatest demon lurking to steal and stifle our growth is fear. Fear abounds in degrees and levels that are unfathomable. The problem is that we give it free reign over our spirits and our hearts, allowing it the privilege of sapping and sucking our energy. We need to believe we can and do have control over it. If we don't, we'll never grow.

Bullied Into Submission—If we can't generate enough fear on our own, insensitive, insecure tyrants add to our fear through intimidation and bullying tactics. These masters of vile invade— with our permission—our inner selves, killing precious pieces of our confidence. This spirit killer makes it very difficult to grow because we are robbed of the confidence that allows such growth.

Laziness—Laziness seeks the easy way. Growth is not easy. It requires introspection and reflection on some difficult subject matters. It then requires us to change. It is easier not to change. If we let laziness win, perhaps our life will be easy, but it will also be stagnant.

Inner Inertia—Sometimes people do all the right things to develop themselves. They reflect, seek truth, seek the required change. Perhaps they even begin the difficult journey of change. Then, they get stuck and stay stuck. After that, they just hang in a state of limbo. They can't pry themselves loose. They're just like a cat stuck in a tree, only there's no fire department to call.

Ignoring Truth—We have honed our ability to ignore truth. We hear it, but we readily reject it as untruth. We find reason to dismiss it quickly and painlessly, before it can enter and be considered in any depth.

Adapted from *In Search of Honor: Lessons From Workers on How to Build Trust,* by Adele B. Lynn (Belle Vernon, Pa.: BajonHouse Publishing, 1998)

As the coach/trainer, your role is to help the participants see if any of these spirit killers may be stunting their growth. Everyone succumbs to these spirit killers sometimes, but when these spirit killers are frequently present, we are not able to grow. Emotionally intelligent leaders confront these spirit killers and move on. As the coach/trainer, your role is to help participants move past these destructive positions.

TRAINER'S/COACH'S NOTES

	APPROXIMATE TIME

1. Overview

5 minutes

Explain to the individual or group that they can be robbed of lifelong learning experience by certain spirit killers that stunt growth. Explain that the emotionally intelligent leader learns to recognize blocks to her growth and works to overcome them. The six most common spirit killers that block our growth are:

- Celebrity ego
- Fear
- Bullied into submission by someone
- Laziness
- Inner inertia
- Ignoring truth.

These six spirit killers, however, can be overcome by leaders who constantly work to improve themselves. The first step to overcoming these spirit killers, however, is to understand and recognize them.

2. Purpose

1 minute

"The purpose of this exercise is to help you recognize and understand the top six spirit killers that can stunt your growth and rob you of your potential to be a truly great leader. The awareness step is vital to continuing your development as a leader. Also, awareness is central to emotional intelligence. In this exercise, it is our intention to help you identify the spirit killers that may be at work to stunt your growth so that you can then develop strategies for dealing effectively with them."

3. Give Directions

20 minutes

A. Give the participants Exercise #46.

B. Instruct participants to complete the worksheet by placing a check mark on the spirit killers that sometimes stunt their growth.

C. Also, ask the participants to think about how to prevent these spirit killers from stunting their growth.

4. Debrief by asking the following questions:

25 minutes

A. When you consider the spirit killers listed, is there a pattern of one or two that prove most destructive for you?

B. What do you think you could do to diminish the impact of the spirit killers?

C. Who could help you overcome the obstacles that can stunt your growth?

D. What would you gain if you could erase these spirit killers from your life?

Emotional Intelligence Exercise 46

Spirit Killers and Soul Suckers—Listed below are the major spirit killers that keep leaders from growing. Put a check mark next to the items that may sometimes stunt your growth.

☐ Celebrity ego

☐ Fear

☐ Bullied into submission by someone

☐ Laziness

☐ Inner inertia

☐ Ignoring truth

What can you do to prevent these spirit killers from robbing your development?

EQ #47 / **Your Most Inspired Self**

EQ TARGET

✓	**Self-Awareness and Control**
	Empathy
	Social Expertness
	Personal Influence
✓	**Mastery of Vision**

OBJECTIVES

- To deepen participants' self-confidence and self-awareness

- To help participants appreciate their best leadership qualities and to feel grateful for these qualities.

ESTIMATED TIME

60 minutes

MATERIALS

Emotional Intelligence Exercise #47

RISK/DIFFICULTY

High

COACHING TIPS FOR COACH/TRAINER

Within every leader, some form of greatness exists that enables that leader to be a better leader. It is important for leaders to be aware of their greatness in order for them to be able to call on these qualities when they need them the most.

By acknowledging greatness and calling it to the leader's attention, she becomes better able to find it in times of need. Also, when leaders interact with others by using their greatness, the end result is usually an authentic interaction that others can appreciate and value.

This exercise asks leaders to write a letter to their most inspired self. It asks the leader to find within herself those qualities that are most inspiring. Also, by acknowledging these qualities, you are forcing the leader to bring them to the surface, which keeps them handy for all to see.

The coach's role is to validate the leader's strength. Coaches should encourage honest validation of strengths. This exercise can also serve as a validation for career choices. It is possible, however, for some participants to realize that their true strengths are not directly connected to the present job they are performing or are not aligned with the organization in which they currently work. If this is the scenario, the coach should not ignore these expressions of honesty.

TRAINER'S/COACH'S NOTES

	APPROXIMATE TIME

1. Overview

1 minute

Explain to the individual or group that it is important to express and validate their most treasured gifts. Each leader has certain qualities or skills that when tapped are truly an expression of her greatness. However, it is also true that leaders may not stop and honor these gifts. When they honor their true gifts, they become better leaders because they put their gifts out to be used by others in a productive way. Emotionally intelligent leaders know where they can make a difference. Usually leaders are most satisfied and most effective when "playing" to their most inspired self—that component that is natural, comfortable, and great.

2. Purpose

5 minutes

"The purpose of this exercise is to help you to appreciate and honor your most inspired self. Each leader has within herself a great leader. That great leader has qualities and characteristics which, when allowed to shine through, become inspiring to others. The leader who is aware of her greatness and honors and allows it to show itself contributes on a much higher level. Don't confuse this with egotism. This isn't about considering yourself great, it is about humbly knowing that part of you that is actually great. When you know this part and call it forth as a leader, others around you become inspired. In this exercise, you will identify and honor your most inspired self. Your most inspired self is that part of you that is naturally gifted as a leader. It is that part that is not strained or stressed over the duties of leadership, but instead, it is the natural, easy part of leadership that you are good at and others recognize easily and find inspiring. It is that voice within you that is true brilliance as a leader. It is when you know that you are performing just perfectly. Of course, most people are not at that level all the time, but the more often you can be there, the better your performance. However, most leaders find that often in only a small percentage of their time can they come from this special place. Leaders often complain that they are limited by organizational realities and other factors that interfere with their ability to be their most inspired self."

3. Give Directions

30 minutes

    A. Give the participants Exercise #47.

    B. Instruct each participant to write a letter to their most inspired self. Allow individuals time to reflect in private on this exercise.

4. Debrief by asking the following questions:

25 minutes

    A. What qualities do you admire in your most inspired self?

    B. How often do you think you are this most inspired self/leader?

    C. What obstacles keep you from being this leader all the time?

D. What do you think people around you think or feel when you are acting from your most inspired self?

E. What would you need to do to be at this level of performance more often?

NOTE: Leaders will often discuss organizational "fit" issues during the debriefing. In reality, sometimes organizations can and do limit the leader's ability to lead. However, it is also possible that it is the leader's perception that the organization places limits, when in reality, this may or may not be true. You should be prepared for a discussion that could help leaders negotiate their way within the present organization or even to launch a career coaching discussion at this point if necessary.

Emotional Intelligence Exercise 47

Write a letter to your most inspired self. Tell your most inspired self what you see that you admire. Tell your most inspired self why you would like to work for him/her. Thank your most inspired self for his/her greatness.

EQ #48 / # Your Leadership Coat of Arms

EQ TARGET

✓	**Self-Awareness and Control**
	Empathy
	Social Expertness
	Personal Influence
✓	**Mastery of Vision**

OBJECTIVES

- To deepen participants' self-awareness and leadership philosophy
- To help participants gain identity as a leader.

ESTIMATED TIME

40 minutes

MATERIALS

Emotional Intelligence Exercise #48

RISK/DIFFICULTY

High

COACHING TIPS FOR COACH/TRAINER

In ancient times, the *coat of arms* was an emblem that represented an individual, family, or country. The symbols on the coat of arms represented and identified the individual, family, or country. These symbols were as diverse as the individuals, families, or countries and represented their spirit and values.

Each leader has certain things that they value and view as significant and important. These items become their hallmark of leadership—they become the things that they stand for as leaders. As a person's leadership philosophy develops, these items become more and more significant and guide the leader's vision of who they are as leaders.

It is worthwhile for leaders to consider the items that most represent what they stand for as a leader. This exercise allows leaders to develop a *coat of arms* that graphically displays what they value most as a leader.

The graphic representation helps solidify what the leader believes in and serves as an important reminder of what he values most in leadership. The coat of arms can also be a reminder of the type of leader and leadership qualities that the leader aspires to become.

In this exercise, your role as the coach is to understand the significance of the leader's choices and to challenge the leader to live up to the symbols. Occasionally you may need to help leaders think visually about the characteristics they find most important. You should be prepared to have examples of visual representations of leadership characteristics and values.

TRAINER'S/COACH'S NOTES

	APPROXIMATE TIME

1. Overview

2 minutes

Explain to the individual or group that it is very important for leaders to know what they value. Emotionally intelligent leaders know what is important to them. They do not borrow someone else's leadership style. They instead have a well-developed sense of what they stand for. Explain that in ancient times, the *coat of arms* was an emblem that represented an individual, family, or country. The symbols on the coat of arms represented and identified the individual, family, or country. These symbols were as diverse as the individuals, families, or countries and represented their spirit and values.

Explain that each leader has certain things that they value and view as significant and important. These items become their hallmark of leadership—they become the things that the leader stands for. As their leadership philosophy develops, these items become more and more significant and guide their vision of who they are as leaders.

2. Purpose

1 minute

"The purpose of this exercise is to help you to develop your leadership philosophy by visualizing a coat of arms that represents who you are as a leader.

It is worthwhile for you to consider the items that most represent what you stand for as a leader. This exercise allows you to develop a coat of arms that graphically displays what you value most as a leader.

The graphic representation helps solidify what you believe in, and it serves as an important reminder of what you value most in leadership. The coat of arms can also be a reminder of the type of leader and leadership qualities that you aspire to."

3. Give Directions

30 minutes

    A. Give the participants Exercise #48.

    B. Instruct each participant to draw a coat of arms that represents the most important items that symbolize what they value in leadership.

NOTE: This exercise is often done on large posters or flip chart paper, making it visible to the class. Encourage participants not to be concerned about artistic expression. Stick figures are just fine.

4. Debrief by asking the following questions:

5 minutes per person

    A. What items are on your coat of arms, and what do they represent?

    B. How did you come to value these characteristics or qualities?

Emotional Intelligence Exercise 48

Draw a crest containing four items that symbolize things you consider most important for a leader to possess. For example, your crest may contain fire, representing your belief that a leader must have passion; a lion, representing your belief that a leader must have great strength; ears, representing your belief that a leader must have the ability to listen, etc.

EQ #49

More Reflections

EQ TARGET

✓	**Self-Awareness and Control**
	Empathy
	Social Expertness
	Personal Influence
✓	**Mastery of Vision**

OBJECTIVES

- To deepen participants' self-confidence and self-awareness
- To help participants appreciate their best leadership qualities and to feel grateful for these qualities.

ESTIMATED TIME

60 minutes

MATERIALS

Emotional Intelligence Exercise #49

RISK/DIFFICULTY

High

COACHING TIPS FOR COACH/TRAINER

Leaders who are confident and self-assured know what they value in terms of leadership. They know what is important, and they have a well-developed personal philosophy of leadership.

Reflection on the type of leader that one hopes to become is very important to development. Reflection helps leaders to sort through what they believe is important. Emotionally competent leaders draw on these beliefs and because of this appear self-confident to those they lead.

Your role as coach is to help leaders determine their beliefs, challenge leaders to test their beliefs against the best practices of leadership that currently exist, and to encourage leaders to live up to their philosophies.

In leaders who are very junior, you may need to suggest readings, courses, or additional discussions that will help the leaders solidify their philosophy of leadership.

TRAINER'S/COACH'S NOTES

	APPROXIMATE TIME

1. Overview
1 minute

Explain to the individual or group that it is important to reflect on leadership to determine the leadership philosophies that are important to the leader.

Explain that reflection aids self-confidence and solidifies and validates what is most important to the leader. Also explain that emotionally intelligent leaders have well-defined leadership philosophies that are a source of strength for the leader.

2. Purpose
2 minutes

"The purpose of this exercise is to help you to reflect on the characteristics that you value most as a leader. By reflecting on what is important to you, you will gain confidence in your leadership decisions and will display that confidence to others. These questions help you to look at leadership from a distance and from the point of view of others. They serve as a tool to help you articulate those qualities that you attribute to great leadership. Also, in the fast pace of the business world, you often are not permitted the luxury of reflection. Therefore, this exercise allows you the freedom to create your philosophy without the rush of getting the job done."

3. Give Directions
25 minutes

A. Give the participants Exercise #49.

B. Instruct each participant to answer the questions on the handout. Allow individuals time to reflect in private on this exercise.

4. Debrief by asking the following questions:
30 minutes

A. What consistencies did you find in your answers?

B. Did you find inconsistencies in your answers? Please elaborate.

C. Would you be pleased if you became the leader whom you reflected on? Why?

D. What obstacles keep you from being this leader?

E. How can you remove these obstacles?

Emotional Intelligence Exercise 49

Imagine that it is 10 years from now and you no longer work at your organization. A group of your former employees are gathered for some refreshments and begin to reminisce about when they used to work for you. What would they have to say about you?

_____

_____

_____

Imagine that it is your funeral and someone steps forward to eulogize you. It is a person who says you were the best boss she ever had. What would she say about you?

_____

_____

_____

If you had a magic wand that could help you become a better leader, what would you do with it?

_____

_____

_____

When you are 80 years old and reflecting back on your life as a leader, what regrets do you think you will have?

_____

_____

_____

EQ #50

The Power of Pictures

EQ TARGET

✓	Self-Awareness and Control
	Empathy
	Social Expertness
	Personal Influence
✓	Mastery of Vision

OBJECTIVES

- To help participants visualize the leadership philosophy and values that they consider most important

- To boost the leaders' self-confidence regarding their leadership voice.

ESTIMATED TIME

50 minutes

MATERIALS

Poster Board
Magazines
Glue Sticks
Magic Markers

RISK/DIFFICULTY

Low

COACHING TIPS FOR COACH/TRAINER

The task of leading a team and inspiring others to be their best demands that the leader know precisely what they expect from their team. All team members must know how they are expected to work together to be contributing members of the team. Most importantly, the leader must have a vision of what team and team spirit mean to her.

The leader who can articulate her vision of "team and team spirit" to her team is at a strong advantage over her peers who cannot. Therefore, this exercise is aimed at assisting leaders by creating a visual image of the concept of "team."

Again, by using visual images, the leader develops a strong sense or picture of what she values most related to the concepts of team and team spirit.

This exercise asks leaders to find images in magazines or discarded posters or books that speak to their philosophy of how people should work together. The leader will create a visual roadmap that will take into consideration the values and significance of working together to get things done. This visual roadmap is an extension of the leader's philosophy about leading people to be their best.

An extension of this exercise can be used with the leader's team. Several variations of this exercise can help the leader and the team articulate their vision for working together.

This exercise is especially useful after the leader has established her own philosophy of leadership and is looking for a way to share that philosophy with her team. It is also useful for team building and sharing common vision.

TRAINER'S/COACH'S NOTES

	APPROXIMATE TIME

1. Overview

Explain to the individual or group that it is the task of leading or inspiring others that requires the leader to know precisely what she expects from her team.

All team members must know how they are expected to work together to be contributing members of the team. Most importantly, the leader must have a vision of what team and team spirit mean to her.

The leader who can articulate her vision of "team and team spirit" to her team is at a strong advantage over her peers who cannot. Therefore, this exercise is aimed at assisting leaders by creating a visual image of the concept of "team."

1 minute

2. Purpose

"The purpose of this exercise is to help you to develop and articulate your vision of team and team spirit to your people. By using visual images, you will develop a strong sense or picture of what you value most and how that relates to the concepts of team and team spirit.

This exercise asks you to find images in magazines or discarded posters or books that speak to your philosophy of how people should work together. You will create a visual roadmap that will take into consideration the values and significance of working together to get things done. This roadmap is an extension of your philosophy about leading people to be their best."

2 minutes

3. Give Directions

A. Give the participants the following supplies:

Magazines

Glue Stick

Poster Board

Magic Markers

B. Instruct the participants to search through the magazines for pictures and images that capture their attention. Images can be positive or negative ones that associate feelings related to work and teams. These images should somehow confirm something that the leader believes about teams and team spirit.

C. Ask the participants to glue the images to the poster board.

D. If appropriate, the magic markers can be used to label themes or other values that the pictures represent.

E. Allow individuals time to reflect on their poster board creations.

40 minutes

4. Debrief by asking each participant the following questions: **10 minutes per person**

   A. Explain your selections. What images did you select and what do the images represent to you?

   B. What can you gain by sharing these images with your team members?

   C. What obstacles keep you from being the kind of team depicted in your pictures or having the type of team spirit depicted in your pictures?

   D. What can you do to overcome these obstacles?

Additional Ideas

The exercises in this book can be used in a variety of different curriculums. Emotional intelligence is a fundamental factor in many workplace skills. Therefore, as coaches and trainers, you are encouraged to adapt and use these exercises when teaching or facilitating communication skills, team building, interpersonal skills, and any variety of leadership or supervisory training.

Use the guides below to select exercises that are most appropriate for your needs. Since the exercises are written for developing leaders, in each case, you will need to substitute peer, coworker, team member, or other noun that describes the target.

EMOTIONAL INTELLIGENCE ACTIVITIES FOR DEVELOPING COMMUNICATION SKILLS
(Substitute the word "coworker" for leader when facilitating these exercises.)

Emotional Intelligence Activity	Page Number	Risk/Difficulty	Emotional Intelligence Competencies				
			Self-Awareness/ Control	Empathy	Social Expertness	Personal Influence	Mastery of Vision
1. Champion or Chump	15	M	✓		✓		
9. Coming Through	55	H	✓	✓			
11. Listening Habits	65	M	✓	✓	✓		
12. Genuine Listening	71	L	✓	✓	✓		
13. Tuning In to Our Employees	75	M	✓	✓	✓		
19. A Note of Thanks	107	H	✓	✓	✓	✓	
46. Spirit Killers That Stunt Your Growth	246	H	✓				✓
47. Your Most Inspired Self	247	H	✓				✓
48. Your Leadership Coat of Arms	253	H	✓				✓
49. More Reflections	257	H	✓				✓

EMOTIONAL INTELLIGENCE ACTIVITIES FOR DEVELOPING TEAM BUILDING
(Substitute the words "team member" for leader when facilitating these exercises.)

Emotional Intelligence Activity	Page Number	Risk/Difficulty	Emotional Intelligence Competencies				
			Self-Awareness/ Control	Empathy	Social Expertness	Personal Influence	Mastery of Vision
1. Champion or Chump	15	M	✓		✓		
7. Personality Contest	45	L	✓	✓	✓	✓	
8. Music of Our Workplace	49	M		✓	✓	✓	✓
9. Coming Through	55	H	✓	✓			
11. Listening Habits	65	M	✓	✓	✓		
12. Genuine Listening	71	L	✓	✓	✓		
13. Tuning In to Our Employees	75	M	✓	✓	✓		
14. I Was Appreciated	79	L	✓		✓	✓	
16. Gifts	91	L			✓	✓	
19. A Note of Thanks	107	H	✓	✓	✓	✓	
20. Dumped On	113	M		✓			✓
25. I Value, We Value	141	M	✓			✓	✓
27. You Expect Me to What?	151	H	✓	✓		✓	
45. Steps for Growth	237	H	✓				✓
46. Spirit Killers That Stunt Your Growth	246	H	✓				✓
48. Your Leadership Coat of Arms	253	H	✓				✓
50. The Power of Pictures	261	L	✓				✓

EMOTIONAL INTELLIGENCE ACTIVITIES FOR DEVELOPING INTERPERSONAL SKILLS
(Substitute the word "peer" for leader when facilitating these exercises.)

Emotional Intelligence Activity	Page Number	Risk/Difficulty	Emotional Intelligence Competencies				
			Self-Awareness/ Control	Empathy	Social Expertness	Personal Influence	Mastery of Vision
1. Champion or Chump	15	M	✓		✓		
2. Importance Meter	19	L	✓	✓	✓		
3. Adding Fuel to the Importance Meter	25	L		✓	✓	✓	
6. Picture Yourself	41	L			✓		✓
7. Personality Contest	45	L	✓	✓	✓	✓	
8. Music of Our Workplace	49	M		✓	✓	✓	✓
9. Coming Through	55	H	✓	✓			
11. Listening Habits	65	M	✓	✓	✓		
12. Genuine Listening	71	L	✓	✓	✓		
13. Tuning In to Our Employees	75	M	✓	✓	✓		
14. I Was Appreciated	79	L	✓		✓	✓	
19. A Note of Thanks	107	H	✓	✓	✓	✓	
45. Steps for Growth	237	H	✓				✓
46. Spirit Killers That Stunt Your Growth	246	H	✓				✓
47. Your Most Inspired Self	247	H	✓				✓
48. Your Leadership Coat of Arms	253	H	✓				✓
49. More Reflections	257	H	✓				✓

EMOTIONAL INTELLIGENCE ACTIVITIES FOR DEVELOPING LEADERS/MANAGERS/SUPERVISORS ONLY

Emotional Intelligence Activity	Page Number	Risk/Difficulty	Self-Awareness/ Control	Empathy	Social Expertness	Personal Influence	Mastery of Vision
2. Importance Meter	19	L	✓	✓	✓		
4. Rank Order Your Employees	31	H	✓	✓	✓		
5. Ask for Feedback	37	H	✓	✓	✓		
9. Coming Through	55	H	✓	✓			
10. Open and Friendly Versus Friendship	61	M		✓	✓		✓
15. A Grateful Heart	85	L	✓		✓		
17. Yes, But . . .	97	M					✓
18. Common Mistakes With Gratitude	101	H	✓	✓		✓	
21. Doing a Fair Share	119	H		✓		✓	✓
22. The Boss's Fair Share	125	H	✓	✓		✓	
23. Action/Reaction	131	M	✓	✓		✓	
24. Take A Stand	135	H				✓	✓
26. Contribution Spirit Killers	147	H	✓	✓		✓	
28. Great Vision	155	L	✓			✓	✓
29. My Vision	161	M			✓	✓	✓
30. Inspiring Words	165	H				✓	✓
31. Sharing Your Vision	169	M				✓	✓
32. Who Invents?	173	H	✓			✓	
33. Visions Apply to People Too	179	H	✓		✓	✓	
34. Vision Spirit Killers	185	H	✓	✓		✓	
35. Advice From the Pros	189	L	✓				✓
36. Working Toward the Vision	193	M				✓	✓
37. Advice From Employees	197	H	✓			✓	✓
38. Today's Actions Toward the Vision	203	M				✓	✓

**EMOTIONAL INTELLIGENCE ACTIVITIES FOR DEVELOPING
LEADERS/MANAGERS/SUPERVISORS ONLY
(continued)**

Emotional Intelligence Activity	Page Number	Risk/Difficulty	Emotional Intelligence Competencies				
			Self-Awareness/Control	Empathy	Social Expertness	Personal Influence	Mastery of Vision
39. Fuel the Vision	207	M	✓			✓	
40. Picture Yourself	211	M				✓	✓
41. Lessons From Low Points/High Points	215	H	✓			✓	
42. It's My Show	221	H	✓				✓
43. Interior Power	227	H	✓			✓	✓
44. Control and Empowerment	231	H	✓	✓		✓	

Recommended Resources

Blanchard, Ken, and Michael O'Connor. *Managing by Values*. San Francisco: Berrett-Koehler Publishers, 1997.

Canfield, Jack, and Jacqueline Miller. *Heart at Work: Stories and Strategies for Building Self-Esteem and Reawakening the Soul at Work*. New York: McGraw-Hill, 1996.

Conger, Jay A. *The Charismatic Leader: Behind the Mystique of Exceptional Leadership*. San Francisco: Jossey-Bass Publishers, 1992.

Cooper, Robert K., and Ayman Sawaf. *Executive EQ: Emotional Intelligence in Leadership and Organizations*. New York: The Berkley Publishing Group, 1997.

Covey, Stephen. *Principle-Centered Leadership*. New York: Summit Books, 1990.

Goleman, Daniel. *Emotional Intelligence: Why It Can Matter More Than IQ*. New York: Bantam Books, 1995.

——. *Working with Emotional Intelligence*. New York: Bantam Books, 1998.

Harmon, Frederick G. *Playing for Keeps*. New York: John Wiley & Sons, 1996.

Hawley, Jack. *Reawakening the Spirit in Work*. New York: Simon & Schuster, 1995.

Herman, Stanley M. *The Tao at Work: On Leading and Following*. San Francisco: Jossey-Bass Publishers, 1994.

Jones, Laurie Beth. *Jesus CEO: Using Ancient Wisdom for Visionary Leadership*. New York: Hyperion, 1995.

Kaye, Les. *Zen at Work*. New York: Crown Trade Paperbacks, 1996.

Kelley, Robert E. *How to be a Star at Work*. New York: Times Business, Random House, 1998.

Kouzes, James, and Barry Posner. *The Leadership Challenge*. San Francisco: Jossey-Bass Publishers, 1987.

Lynn, Adele B. *In Search of Honor: Lessons From Workers on How to Build Trust*. Belle Vernon, Pa.: BajonHouse Publishing, 1998.

Salovey, Peter, and John Mayer. *Emotional Development and Emotional Intelligence*. New York: Basic Books, 1997.

Sashkin, Marshall. *Becoming a Visionary Leader*. King of Prussia, Pa.: Organization Design and Development, 1986.

Sterrett, Emily. *The Manager's Pocket Guide to Emotional Intelligence*. Amherst, Mass.: HRD Press, 2000.

Weisinger, Hendrie. *Emotional Intelligence at Work*. San Francisco: Jossey-Bass Publishers, 1998.

Index

Action/Reaction activity, 131–134
Adding Fuel to Importance Meter activity, 25–29
Advice from Employees activity, 197–201
Advice from the Pros activity, 189–192
Advice Giver listening pattern, 66
Ask for Feedback activity, 37–40
assessment
    coach/trainer role in, 5, 7
    self-assessment, 7, 37–40

belief systems
    coach/trainer role in, 5
    converting to productive behavior, 5
    creating, 5
    It's My Show activity, 221–225
    I Value, We Value activity, 141–145
    More Reflections activity, 257–260
    Take A Stand activity, 135–139
    Your Leadership Coat of Arms activity, 253–256
blind gratitude, 102
The Boss's Fair Share activity, 125–129
bullying, as spirit killer, 244

caring, Open and Friendly vs. Friendship activity, 61–64
celebrity ego, as spirit killer, 244
Champion or Chump activity, 15–18
Cherniss, Cary, 3
coach/trainer, role in emotional intelligence, 5, 7
collaboration, see team building
Coming Through activity, 55–59
commitment toward goals
    Advice from Employees activity, 197–201
    Contribution Spirit Killers activity, 147–150
    Great Vision activity, 155–159
    Take A Stand activity, 135–139

Today's Actions Toward the Vision activity, 203–206
    Vision Spirit Killers activity, 185–188
    Working Toward the Vision activity, 193–196
Common Mistakes with Gratitude activity, 101–106
communication skills development, 266
    Champion or Chump activity, 15–18
    Coming Through activity, 55–59
    Genuine Listening activity, 71–74
    Listening Habits activity, 65–69
    More Reflections activity, 257–260
    A Note of Thanks activity, 107–111
    Spirit Killers That Stunt Your Growth activity, 243–246
    Tuning In to Our Employees activity, 75–78
    Your Leadership Coat of Arms activity, 253–256
    Your Most Inspired Self activity, 247–251
conflict resolution, 3–4
congruence
    It's My Show activity, 221–225
    I Value, We Value activity, 141–145
    Take a Stand activity, 135–139
Consortium for Research on Emotional Intelligence in Organizations, 3
Contribution Spirit Killers activity, 147–150
Control and Empowerment activity, 231–235
Cooper, Robert K., 1
cooperation, see team building
corporate culture, Music of Our Workplace activity, 49–54
critical thinking, A Grateful Heart activity, 85–89

debriefing exercises, 8
Doing a Fair Share activity, 119–124
Dumped On activity, 113–117

egotism, as spirit killer, 244
emotional intelligence (EQ)
  business case for, 2–3
  coach/trainer role in, 5, 7
  framework for, 3–4
  IQ versus, 2
  nature of, 1
  working definition, 2–3
empathy
  Action/Reaction activity, 131–134
  Adding Fuel to Importance Meter activity,
    25–29
  Ask for Feedback activity, 37–40
  The Boss's Fair Share activity, 125–129
  Coming Through activity, 55–59
  Common Mistakes with Gratitude activity,
    101–106
  Contribution Spirit Killers activity, 147–150
  Control and Empowerment activity, 231–235
  described, 3
  Doing a Fair Share activity, 119–124
  Dumped On activity, 113–117
  Genuine Listening activity, 71–74
  Importance Meter activity, 19–29
  Listening Habits activity, 65–69
  Music of Our Workplace activity, 49–54
  A Note of Thanks activity, 107–111
  Open and Friendly vs. Friendship activity,
    61–64
  Personality Contest activity, 45–48
  Rank Order Your Employees activity, 31–35
  self-awareness and control, 185–188
  Tuning In to Our Employees activity, 75–78
  You Expect Me to What? activity, 151–154
Executive EQ (Cooper and Sawaf), 1
extroversion, 8

fairness
  The Boss's Fair Share activity, 125–129
  Doing a Fair Share activity, 119–124
  Dumped On activity, 113–117
Faker listening pattern, 66
fear, as spirit killer, 244
Fuel the Vision activity, 207–210

Genuine Listening activity, 71–74
Gifts activity, 91–95

Goleman, Daniel, 1
A Grateful Heart activity, 85–89
gratitude
  Common Mistakes with Gratitude activity,
    101–106
  Gifts activity, 91–95
  A Grateful Heart activity, 85–89
  I Was Appreciated activity, 79–83
  More Reflections activity, 257–260
  A Note of Thanks activity, 107–111
  Yes, But . . . activity, 97–100
Great Vision activity, 155–159

Happy Hooker listening pattern, 66
High difficulty factor, 7
honesty, Common Mistakes with Gratitude ac-
    tivity, 101–106
How to Be a Star at Work (Kelley), 1

ignoring truth, as spirit killer, 244
Importance Meter activity, 19–29
  Adding Fuel to Importance Meter activity,
    25–29
  basic activity, 19–24
importance of self
  Adding Fuel to Importance Meter activity,
    25–29
  Champion or Chump activity, 15–18
  Importance Meter activity, 19–29
  Rank Order Your Employees activity, 31–35
inner inertia, as spirit killer, 244
In Search of Honor (Lynn), 1, 102–103, 147–
    148, 185–186, 198, 207–208, 243–244
insincere gratitude, 102
Inspiring Words activity, 165–168
Intellectual listening pattern, 66
Interior Power activity, 227–230
interpersonal skills development, 268
  Adding Fuel to Importance Meter activity,
    25–29
  Champion or Chump activity, 15–18
  Coming Through activity, 55–59
  Genuine Listening activity, 71–74
  Importance Meter activity, 19–29
  I Was Appreciated activity, 79–83
  Listening Habits activity, 65–69

More Reflections activity, 257–260
Music of Our Workplace activity, 49–54
A Note of Thanks activity, 107–111
Personality Contest activity, 45–48
Picture Yourself activity, 41–44
Spirit Killers That Stunt Your Growth activity, 243–246
Steps for Growth activity, 237–242
Tuning In to Our Employees activity, 75–78
Your Leadership Coat of Arms activity, 253–256
Your Most Inspired Self activity, 247–251
Interrupter listening pattern, 66
introversion, 8
It's My Show activity, 221–225
I Value, We Value activity, 141–145
I Was Appreciated activity, 79–83

Kelley, Robert E., 1

laziness, as spirit killer, 244
leadership development, 7, 269
    Action/Reaction activity, 131–134
    Advice from Employees activity, 197–201
    Advice from the Pros activity, 189–192
    Ask for Feedback activity, 37–40
    The Boss's Fair Share activity, 125–129
    Coming Through activity, 55–59
    Common Mistakes with Gratitude activity, 101–106
    Contribution Spirit Killers activity, 147–150
    Control and Empowerment activity, 231–235
    Doing a Fair Share activity, 119–124
    Fuel the Vision activity, 207–210
    A Grateful Heart activity, 85–89
    Great Vision activity, 155–159
    Importance Meter activity, 19–29
    Inspiring Words activity, 165–168
    Interior Power activity, 227–230
    It's My Show activity, 221–225
    Lessons from Low Points/High Points activity, 215–219
    My Vision activity, 161–164
    Open and Friendly vs. Friendship activity, 61–64
    Picture Yourself activity, 41–44

Rank Order Your Employees activity, 31–35
Sharing Your Vision activity, 169–172
Take A Stand activity, 135–139
Today's Actions Toward the Vision activity, 203–206
Visions Apply to People Too activity, 179–183
Vision Spirit Killers activity, 185–188
Who Invents activity, 173–177
Working Toward the Vision activity, 193–196
Yes, But . . . activity, 97–100
learning styles, 8
Lessons from Low Points/High Points activity, 215–219
Listening Habits activity, 65–69
listening skills
    Ask for Feedback activity, 37–40
    Genuine Listening activity, 71–74
    Listening Habits activity, 65–69
    mindset for, 71–72, 75–76
    negative listening patterns, 66
    Tuning In to Our Employees activity, 75–78
Logical listening pattern, 66
L'Oreal, 2–3
Low risk/difficulty factor, 7
Lynn, Adele B., 1

manager development, see leadership development
mastery of vision
    Advice from Employees activity, 197–201
    Advice from the Pros activity, 189–192
    Common Mistakes with Gratitude activity, 101–106
    described, 4
    Doing a Fair Share activity, 119–124
    Dumped On activity, 113–117
    Great Vision activity, 155–159
    Inspiring Words activity, 165–168
    Interior Power activity, 227–230
    It's My Show activity, 221–225
    I Value, We Value activity, 141–145
    More Reflections activity, 257–260
    Music of Our Workplace activity, 49–54
    My Vision activity, 161–164
    Open and Friendly vs. Friendship activity, 61–64

mastery of vision (*continued*)
Picture Yourself activity, 41–44, 211–214
The Power of Pictures activity, 261–264
Sharing Your Vision activity, 169–172
Spirit Killers That Stunt Your Growth, 243–246
Steps for Growth activity, 237–242
Take a Stand activity, 135–139
Today's Actions Toward the Vision activity, 203–206
Working Toward the Vision activity, 193–196
Yes, But . . . activity, 97–100
Your Leadership Coat of Arms activity, 253–256
Your Most Inspired Self activity, 247–251
Medium difficulty factor, 7
mixed messages
It's My Show activity, 221–225
I Value, We Value activity, 141–145
Take a Stand activity, 135–139
monetary rewards, gratitude and, 102
More Reflections activity, 257–260
Music of Our Workplace activity, 49–54
Myers-Briggs type scales, 8
My Vision activity, 161–164

negative feelings
Contribution Spirit Killers activity, 147–150
Dumped On activity, 113–117
Importance Meter activity, 19–29
Rank Order Your Employees activity, 31–35
Visions Apply to People Too activity, 179–183
A Note of Thanks activity, 107–111

Open and Friendly vs. Friendship activity, 61–64
organizational culture, Music of Our Workplace activity, 49–54

past experiences
Champion or Chump activity, 15–18
impact of leader on followers, 15–18
I Was Appreciated activity, 79–83
Lessons from Low Points/High Points activity, 215–219
personal influence
Action/Reaction activity, 131–134

Adding Fuel to Importance Meter activity, 25–29
Advice from Employees activity, 197–201
The Boss's Fair Share activity, 125–129
Common Mistakes with Gratitude activity, 101–106
Contribution Spirit Killers activity, 147–150
Control and Empowerment activity, 231–235
described, 4
Doing a Fair Share activity, 119–124
Fuel the Vision activity, 207–210
Gifts activity, 91–95
Great Vision activity, 155–159
Inspiring Words activity, 165–168
Interior Power activity, 227–230
I Value, We Value activity, 141–145
I Was Appreciated activity, 79–83
Lessons from Low Points/High Points activity, 215–219
Music of Our Workplace activity, 49–54
My Vision activity, 161–164
A Note of Thanks activity, 107–111
Personality Contest activity, 45–48
Picture Yourself activity, 211–214
self-awareness and control, 185–188
Sharing Your Vision activity, 169–172
Take A Stand activity, 135–139
Visions Apply to People Too activity, 179–183
Who Invents? activity, 173–177
Working Toward the Vision activity, 193–196
You Expect Me to What? activity, 151–154
Personality Contest activity, 45–48
Picture Yourself activity, 41–44, 211–214
positive feelings
Action/Reaction activity, 131–134
Common Mistakes with Gratitude activity, 101–106
Gifts activity, 91–95
A Grateful Heart activity, 85–89
I Was Appreciated activity, 79–83
Yes, But . . . activity, 97–100
positive reinforcement, coach/trainer role in, 5
The Power of Pictures activity, 261–264
productivity
Contribution Spirit Killers activity, 147–150
Doing a Fair Share activity, 119–124

Dumped On activity, 113–117
impact of leaders on followers, 15–18
I Was Appreciated activity, 79–83
Rank Order Your Employees activity, 31–35

Rank Order Your Employees activity, 31–35
Rebuttal Maker listening pattern, 66
redundant gratitude, 102
reinforcement of behavior, 8

Sawaf, Ayman, 1
self-awareness and control
    Action/Reaction activity, 131–134
    Advice from Employees activity, 197–201
    Advice from the Pros activity, 189–192
    Ask for Feedback activity, 37–40
    The Boss's Fair Share activity, 125–129
    Champion or Chump activity, 15–18
    coach/trainer role in, 5
    Coming Through activity, 55–59
    Common Mistakes with Gratitude activity,
        101–106
    Contribution Spirit Killers activity, 147–150
    Control and Empowerment activity, 231–235
    described, 3
    Doing a Fair Share activity, 119–124
    Fuel the Vision activity, 207–210
    Genuine Listening activity, 71–74
    A Grateful Heart activity, 85–89
    Great Vision activity, 155–159
    Importance Meter activity, 19–24
    Interior Power activity, 227–230
    It's My Show activity, 221–225
    I Value, We Value activity, 141–145
    I Was Appreciated activity, 79–83
    Lessons from Low Points/High Points activ-
        ity, 215–219
    Listening Habits activity, 65–69
    More Reflections activity, 257–260
    A Note of Thanks activity, 107–111
    Personality Contest activity, 45–48
    Picture Yourself activity, 211–214
    The Power of Pictures activity, 261–264
    Rank Order Your Employees activity, 31–35
    self-assessment and, 7

    Spirit Killers That Stunt Your Growth,
        243–246
    Steps for Growth activity, 237–242
    Tuning In to Our Employees activity, 75–78
    Visions Apply to People Too activity, 179–183
    Vision Spirit Killers activity, 185–188
    Who Invents? activity, 173–177
    You Expect Me to What? activity, 151–154
    Your Leadership Coat of Arms activity,
        253–256
    Your Most Inspired Self activity, 247–251
Sharing Your Vision activity, 169–172
social expertness
    Adding Fuel to Importance Meter activity,
        25–29
    Ask for Feedback activity, 37–40
    Champion or Chump activity, 15–18
    described, 3–4
    Genuine Listening activity, 71–74
    Gifts activity, 91–95
    A Grateful Heart activity, 85–89
    Importance Meter activity, 19–29
    I Was Appreciated activity, 79–83
    Listening Habits activity, 65–69
    Music of Our Workplace activity, 49–54
    My Vision activity, 161–164
    A Note of Thanks activity, 107–111
    Open and Friendly vs. Friendship activity,
        61–64
    Personality Contest activity, 45–48
    Picture Yourself activity, 41–44
    Rank Order Your Employees activity, 31–35
    Tuning In to Our Employees activity, 75–78
    Visions Apply to People Too activity, 179–183
spirit killers
    Advice from Employees activity, 197–201
    Contribution Spirit Killers activity, 147–150
    lists of, 147–148, 185–186
    Spirit Killers That Stunt Your Growth activity,
        243–246
    Vision Spirit Killers activity, 185–188
Spirit Killers That Stunt Your Growth activity,
    243–246
Steps for Growth activity, 237–242
success
    Picture Yourself activity, 41–44

success (*continued*)
    Spirit Killers That Stunt Your Growth activity, 243–246
    Steps for Growth activity, 237–242
    Your Most Inspired Self activity, 247–251
supervisor development, *see* leadership development

Take A Stand activity, 135–139
team building, 267
    Champion or Chump activity, 15–18
    Coming Through activity, 55–59
    Dumped On activity, 113–117
    Genuine Listening activity, 71–74
    Gifts activity, 91–95
    I Value, We Value activity, 141–145
    I Was Appreciated activity, 79–83
    Listening Habits activity, 65–69
    Music of Our Workplace activity, 49–54
    A Note of Thanks activity, 107–111
    Personality Contest activity, 45–48
    The Power of Pictures activity, 261–264
    Spirit Killers That Stunt Your Growth activity, 243–246
    Steps for Growth activity, 237–242
    Tuning In to Our Employees activity, 75–78
    You Expect Me to What? activity, 151–154
    Your Leadership Coat of Arms activity, 253–256

Today's Actions Toward the Vision activity, 203–206
training formats, 11–13
    Format A—Introduction to EQ, 11
    Format B—EQ Essentials, 11–12
    Format C—EQ Strategies, 12–13
Tuning In to Our Employees activity, 75–78

values in workplace
    It's My Show activity, 221–225
    I Value, We Value activity, 141–145
    More Reflections activity, 257–260
    The Power of Pictures activity, 261–264
    Your Leadership Coat of Arms activity, 253–256
vision, *see* mastery of vision
Visions Apply to People Too activity, 179–183
Vision Spirit Killers activity, 185–188
visualization
    Music of Our Workplace activity, 49–54
    Picture Yourself activity, 41–44, 211–214
    The Power of Pictures activity, 261–264

Who Invents? activity, 173–177
Working Toward the Vision activity, 193–196
Working with Emotional Intelligence (Goleman), 1

Yes, But . . . activity, 97–100
You Expect Me to What? activity, 151–154
Your Leadership Coat of Arms activity, 253–256
Your Most Inspired Self activity, 247–251

CPSIA information can be obtained at www.ICGtesting.com
Printed in the USA
LVOW03s1811110414

381361LV00008B/275/P